GETTING STARTED IN PROPERTY…

What I Wish I'd Known at the Beginning!

by **Kellyann Martin**

CONTENTS

INTRODUCTION INTO PROPERTY: WHAT I DO, AND WHAT YOU'LL LEARN FROM THIS BOOK

I have a frequent joke with all my pals that I have no real skills in life.

I'm not amazingly intelligent, my DIY attempts are shambolic, I have no sense of co-ordination, or manual skills – in fact I promise you in the most open manner possible, because it's no secret – I'm just your ordinary average person.

There's really nothing spectacularly amazing about me.

But, one great facet of my personality is that I try hard, and always do so, consistently.

You will never beat anybody who refuses to give up – and I'm a stubborn bugger for never giving up!

Thus, I've managed to build a property portfolio, where I provide long term residential accommodation for families in my hometown of Leeds.

This portfolio provides me with an income and investment assets – despite me initially having no skills, knowledge or money to do so.
Good stuff, eh?!?

But I'm really nowt special.

I've just learnt and followed a process, and followed guidance from the best people in the industry. And tried consistently.

Now I've made a decent success of it, I'm in a position to help other new people start their property career as well – and a key way to get cracking is by reading this book, so you've made a good start!

So although this book is property-based, it's not going to be teaching you 'how' to do property: strategies, business models, housing markets, doing deals etc... there's tons of other books which will cover that content.

I wish I'd known so many of these teachings I'm about to share with you at the beginning of my property career – which would have made the process go so much easier, smoother, slicker, faster

.

Hindsight's a wonderful thing, isn't it?!

So, in the words of Oasis: there are many things that I would like to say to you...but I *do* know how, that's the difference!

Enjoy your book, it will give you some food for thought about the property industry you're getting into… because it's not as easy as people make out, and it really isn't all sunshine and roses, you know!

Kellyann Martin

CAN ANYONE DO PROPERTY?

We'll start off with some brutal Yorkshire honesty.

I used to think that anybody would be able to do property,

But now I've been in the industry a few years, I've changed my mind.

Hey, it's ok to change your opinion about anything, based on new information!

And if by reading this book, you'll have worked out that actually, perhaps property isn't for you, then at least I'll have saved you the time, effort, hassle, drama, sleepless nights, and of course, spending lots of money.

So having learnt more and experienced more, I have come to this conclusion:

Being in property is not for everybody.

You need to have a certain set of characteristics and traits in order to do well in property.

When I think of the vast amount of people that I've met over the years, who have been all keen and eager to get cracking in property…

...And then I think of the ones that have actually stuck with it and made it work for them, sadly, it is only a fraction of people who have stuck it out.

And that's because the truth is property is hard - despite what you might have been taught on some educational training course.

It really isn't for everyone.

It is hard work, stressful, frustrating, and certainly isn't the 'get rich quick' scheme that you were led to believe!

So here's a few key attributes that I believe you should have if you're seriously considering investing in property as a long-term career.

Key Attributes Required:

A positive nature.

I'll be honest with you here, the majority of days in property aren't that great. You might get up to 10 really good days a year in property (new keys, refurb complete, new tenants), the rest are only average days or bad ones.

Take into account refurbishment problems, tenant or rent problems, and maintenance problems, and then acknowledge that these are all regular problems that occur on a regular basis.

You've got to have a naturally positive nature to avoid being dragged down, discouraged and downhearted by these issues.

Resilience.

It's very important that you are able to recover quickly from difficult situations. When things go wrong, some people bury their head in the sand and avoid problems, which is not the way to go in property.

If you run away and hide from issues in property, you often make the situation worse - such as accruing rent arrears from a naughty tenant, or a leak which may then get worse and destroy the entire property.

You've also got to have "bounce-back-ability" - the ability to keep going even when things have gone wrong.

A thick skin.

Things do go wrong in property… often.

You shouldn't allow yourself to get too upset by them, or take things personally, as that is a sure-fire way to make the situation worse, when emotions get involved.

Try to think logically about problems, even though they may be frustrating and not your fault.

Keep a cool head at all times, and remain impartial. It is pointless to wallow emotionally and be upset thinking "Why has this happened to me? / Why is the tenant behaving in this awful way to me?" It's nothing personal, as it's likely to be nothing to do with you!

Tenacity and Determination.

It is crucial that you have a nature that doesn't give up easily. You must never stop trying to improve or fix things, and you must do whatever is required to fix a goal.

This is especially important if you work for yourself, because you are fully responsible for your property and business - and no one is going to come and save you.

I mean that in the loosest possible terms; obviously maintenance contractors and advisors can help you fix certain things, but you've got to bring about those solutions yourself.

A touch of personal stubbornness helps here, and a willingness to never give up!

👊 Finally, a couple of other traits that are important as a property investor: an ability to **deal effectively with stress, patience, honesty, being proactive, decisive, and having good integrity** - if you always want to do the right thing by your tenants and investors, then you won't go far wrong.

So that's a little insight into some of the key personality traits needed in property. You should ask yourself honestly if you possess all these traits, because if not you will find it more difficult than most.

And if you don't, hey, that's ok too; as I've said, property is not for everybody.

Perhaps you could just focus your skills, time and energy on other things that you love, and invest passively with property developers, without being hands-on.

But if you really wish to get involved with bricks and mortar, vendors, agents, keys, properties, refurbishment, contractors, building materials, expensive problem fixes, tenancies, tenants, and all the associated issues, then I wish my very best of luck to you... because I know how hard it is!

MY TOP FIVE REASONS WHY BEING IN PROPERTY IS GREAT

Still here?!

Still keen to read more?!

Ok, you've had the Scarborough warnings about property, let's move on to why being in property is great.

Here we go...

Number 1: You get to help people.

First and foremost, you are providing homes for tenants. There's a real shortage of rental accommodation, and if you can help provide that service, it benefits both parties.

A great reason to start with!

Number 2: You play the role of magician!

There's something very special about making a superb transformation.

You take an utter grotbox of a house, throw a little magic dust / good contractors / cash and effort at it, et voilá: one great refurbished house!

It feels good to be able to bring dilapidated housing stock back into use.

Nobody wants to see them rot and go to rack and ruin anyway - not in my beautiful Leeds!

Number 3: You only have to do the real hard work once.

I love single let housing.
Once you've done the hard work; i.e., refurbished them to a good standard and rented them out to a lovely tenant, there's actually very little to do.
Yes, there might be the occasional inspection to do, or a couple of times a year the tenant will ring with a maintenance problem that's arisen to be fixed... but on the whole, these rentals just keep ticking away nicely.

What's not to love?!?

Number 4: Property gives you the freedom to do whatever you like!

Looking after a rental portfolio doesn't actually take up a lot of time, meaning you have a good amount of freedom to choose how you spend your time.

And I love doing whatever I like!

Last one!

Number 5: Investors lend you money towards property projects, and you give them a superb return for it.

When I work with private investors, we use a legal loan agreement for the investor to lend me funds to purchase a particular house.

I refurbish the property to a good standard, uplift the value, and place a tenant family in it as their long-term rental home.

Then I put a mortgage on the house, and draw out most of the uplifted equity.

This enables me to repay the investor back their capital, plus a very healthy return - which was much better than anything they can receive in interest from UK high street banks!

Investment funds in this project are returned within 12 months of residential projects.

The investors make a superb profit passively; I helped them, and they help me, and we both help local tenant families!

If you have cash sitting in a bank making poor returns – feel free to get in touch to discuss employing funds in a project just like this to earn you a far better return on investment.

So there we have it, my top five reasons why being in property is great.

Just my own personal opinion of course, and you are all entitled to my own opinion!!

There are plenty more good reasons as well, but that'll do us for now as we move onto the next chapter.

THINGS I WISH I'D LEARNT EARLIER ABOUT PROPERTY INVESTMENT

Nobody can get anywhere in life without making a few mistakes along the way; that's part of the journey!

But if I had known these things earlier in my property investment career, then life would have been a lot easier!

We'll start with the biggie: I should have started investing in property earlier!!

Here's a picture of me aged 23, straight out of teacher training college and in my first English teaching post; a nearby high school - look how fresh-faced, youthful and energetic I look!!

As soon as I started working and earning full-time in teaching, I set about buying the flat I lived in.

I was delighted to discover that the monthly mortgage was much cheaper than the rent I'd been paying!

I still own this flat now, it's rented out and ticks along nicely causing me very little hassle and problems.

So anyway, I'd bought my first property... but then I did nothing else for 10 years!

And for the last 6 of those years, I was the landlord by then... so why didn't I see the opportunity and profit made, and buy more property?!?

WHY WHY WHY?!?!

Hey ho, never mind eh?

We all know that the best time to plant a tree is ten years ago.

The second-best time is NOW.

So get cracking people - don't waste ten years like I did!!

Next item: I wish I'd have realised earlier that other people will lend you money to invest with to create a win-win scenario!

You just read how after buying my own residential property, I did nothing further with property investment for another ten years.

But then I randomly decided to buy another house, and put down the full 25% deposit... and then left it there!!

I had not yet learned about property education, or the magic wonders of the Buy-Refurbish-Refinance model.

And I certainly didn't know that other people would help you buy property, by investing money loans into projects for a great return.

What a great model to have learnt!

Although here's my first house I bought specifically as an investment, still with that 25% deposit trapped in there...

Sometimes you just don't know what you don't know!

Onto the next insight...

One New Year's Day I took the plunge and made the commitment to myself that for my new career, I was going to be a full-time property investor.

I purchased some property training courses, and learnt oh so many wonderful things...

... but then I got distracted by all these wonderful models and strategies: houses of multiple occupancy, no money down deals, lease options, commercial conversions, development, deal sourcing etc etc...

In short, I developed **Shiny Penny Syndrome**, and chased several different things at once!

Now don't get me wrong, I'm not saying these other models are no good; that's not the case - I have many fellow property friends who are doing a great job of making their chosen model work.

I just realised that after studying all these things, refurbishing little Buy-to-Let houses for local families is what I really wanted to do.

Little cheap cheerful houses in Leeds are where my heart lies!

So what I'm saying is, make a general overview study of the property models, and then decide what it is you actually want to invest in, and stick to it!

Learn it inside out; commit time, effort, energy and education to your chosen model...

Don't be chasing anything and everything, here, there and everywhere, shiny penny style!

Because as the old proverb goes: man who chases two rabbits catches none!

Last item of things I wish I'd learnt earlier about property investment!

And yes, I know there's a dozen or more other things I could have picked to talk about, but we're going with this one...

☑ **I wish I'd not been so shy as to offer people investment opportunities!**

You see, I had (and sometimes still have, even now if I'm honest!) a real complex when talking about money.

Growing up, I never borrowed anything off anyone. I never had a credit card until recently. Everything I wanted, I worked hard for, earned money for it and paid for it myself. And if I didn't have the money to afford something then I simply couldn't have it.

So when suddenly I realised I'd have to attract investment from other people, panic struck!

And what would happen was this bizarre scenario, where people would like me and my work, and they would openly say to my face that they would lend me money for investment... and I would go bright red, become embarrassed and awkward, and dance about cringing and fidgeting... in short, do anything to avoid having that conversation about them lending me money - it was crazy!

I had to work really hard to switch my mindset, and to realise that you are helping investors grow their wealth - you are doing them a favour by working together in an opportunity to make more money for them!

I am always flattered and delighted when people offer to lend me money - because it's a massive compliment to know that they know, like and trust you.

And that's a great feeling.

So as long as you are not a wretch who lets people down or rips people off, then you've nothing to worry about.

But even now, I still have to persevere when pitching for investment.

You could say I'm a continuous work in progress!

But as with everything, practice makes perfect!

Secrets Nobody Tells You About Being In Property

After a few years in property, I have discovered a couple of secrets about the Buy-To-Let property industry... I wish I'd known about them sooner!

For some reason, nobody ever tells you about these things at the start of your property career... which would make life much easier for you if you knew them!

Luckily for you property newcomers, I'm going to share these secrets...

Secret Number 1 that nobody tells you about being in property:

The £25,000 salary affordability issue.

Sometimes people new to property investing get a bit keen, quit their job, leave themselves with no salary with the intention of making it big in property.

This is a bad idea!

The reason for this is that a lot of mortgage lenders don't like to provide mortgages for people who have an income of less than £25,000.

Some lenders do; some have no minimum income requirements... but your chances of getting a decent mortgage are much better if you have a salary to begin with.

So rather than suddenly jacking your job in and plunging your salary to zero immediately, a better way to get into property would be this:

Gradually build up your income from property over a couple of years, and gradually decrease the number of days you work in your normal job, so your property income and your job income eventually balance out together into a decent overall salary.

Then one day, your income will solely come from property, as it will surpass your job salary, and you will no longer be exchanging your time working for somebody else!

Secret Number 2 that nobody tells you about being in property:
Help by utilising credit cards and building up lines of credit.

Property is expensive. Most projects cost more than you anticipate, and the cost of refurbishment is what puts a lot of people off doing them.

However, you can get some help to pay for them by utilising credit cards.

Use a low-cost credit card to purchase materials: boilers, kitchens, bathrooms and so on. Yes, they might end up costing you a little more over the long run, but it's better than never doing a project.

Obviously pay down the credit cards as soon as you are able, usually out of the property rental income, once it's up and running.

Build up a couple of lines of credit, with various suppliers too, and this will also help spread the cost.

I always chuckle about this next bit, but how good would it be if you could pay your contractors using a credit card too?!

Most of them want cold hard cash transferring!

But remember: all materials can be bought using credit.

Secret Number 3 that nobody tells you about being in property:
Looking after your credit score.

This is something I'd never even thought about before being in property - but luckily, because I'm of that organised OCD do-things-correctly mindset, I've never done things like miss payments or default on bills.

And here's another fallacy: why should your personal credit record matter if you're buying property in a limited company?

Because it does, and that's all there is to it!

Mortgage lenders want personal guarantees that they're going to get paid, and as limited company directors, that guarantee falls to you - so keep your nose (and credit record!) clean!
Makes sure you pay at least minimum pay amounts every month for bills and credit card payments, in full if you can - and here's the crucial bit: pay them on time; late payments have a detrimental effect on your credit score.

And we want to keep that perfect payment record and score as high as possible - because if lenders think your credit record looks dodgy and you look unreliable, they simply won't lend you money for mortgages!

I check my credit files with different credit agencies a couple of times a month just to ensure all is well - beware other people taking out credit in your name...

I use all three of the Equifax, Experian and Credit Karma credit scoring systems, so get yourselves signed up to one or more of these. The added benefit is they also tell you how to repair and improve your rating.

And everybody loves a high rating - especially mortgage lenders!

Secret Number 4 that nobody tells you about being in property:
Investor difficulties!

A lot of people in property, myself included, leverage funds from private investors to purchase property.
Investors get a great return on their loan investment, and you get help building your portfolio.

Now here's the secret: raising finance is hard. And what makes it harder is that the majority of people who reckon they want to invest funds... simply don't.

Sadly, there's a lot of talkers not walkers, when it comes to investors. I've found people who clearly stated they wanted to lend money out, and then when it came to the crunch... they didn't.

This is for a myriad of reasons, genuine or otherwise:

- they've already lent their money out elsewhere
- they've changed their mind
- they're nervous and scared of the investment process

- they've bought property themselves with their funds.

Or it could be that they simply don't like you and don't want to work with you, or they don't trust you or the deal!

Sometimes, perhaps even they never had the money to begin with and were simply time-wasting tyre-kickers.

Asking for proof of funds here helps weed out the hot-air braggers full of bluster!

The point is this: some people are all talk and no action - so don't just rely on one investor, in case they back out or let you down.

Have a list of "potential investors" lined up who are ready to invest.

Because people only become "investors" if they actually lend you money!

So build those relationships with genuine investors who genuinely want to work with you!

So there you have it... a few inside secrets shared, which hopefully will make your property career much easier for knowing them!

All we want in our property life is happy, safe, low-risk investing,

Steer clear of things – or people – that might cause problems to that aim.

KEEPING COSTS DOWN DURING A HOUSE RENOVATION

At certain times of the year, such as New Year, Spring cleans, Bank Holidays, the lead up to Christmas etc, we Brits traditionally love to decide to have a blitz or redecorate their house - me included, I love doing a few bits and pieces to improve my own house!

A friend once asked me for any tips on renovations for her new house, to keep the budget down.

It caught me a little off guard; because bizarrely it's not something I'm asked often!

But I do have some tips for keeping costs down during refurbishment project, what with being a tight Yorkshire lass and that - and here are a couple, just to assist you with your own houses and investment properties!

KEEPING COSTS DOWN DURING A HOUSE RENOVATION

Make a full list of everything you want to do, and be specific about every job required in every room.

Work out your budget for doing this.

What can be done now, what will have to wait?

What's the priority?

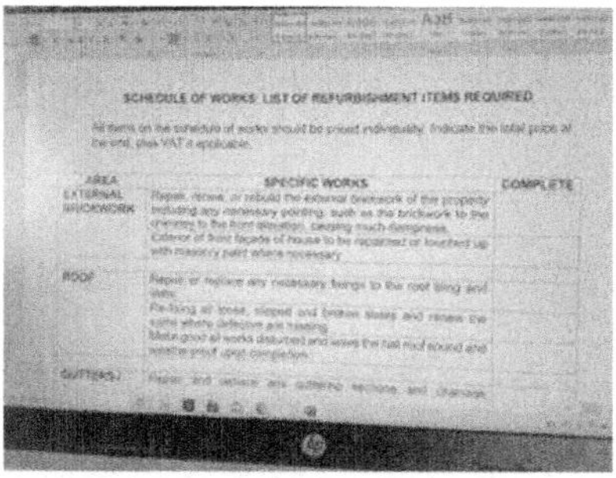

Get any 'big / all over the house' jobs done first, e.g. electrics, plumbing, plastering. Get quotes for any skilled works you need doing (and ALWAYS qualified people for gas and electric work!)

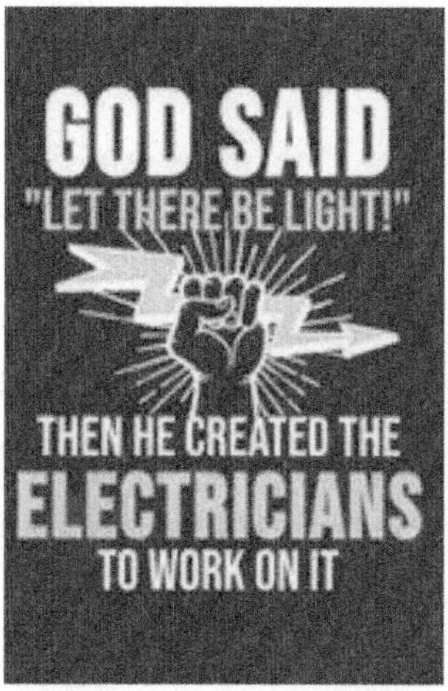

If you're living in the house it whilst you do it up, save your sanity and decide which are the priority areas you'll do first. Don't try and do more than two areas at once whilst living there, unless you can handle a lot of stress, mess and chaos… because on the other hand, living in chaos usually motivates you to do the decorating work in the evenings to get it finished!

Project manage yourself, rather than hire an 'all in one' refurbishment company, who usually charge a premium for this service.

Source individual trades and contractors yourself.

Recommendations of tradespeople are best, from friends that have actually used their services. Read reviews if you're unsure, see their work, or pictures of it, then invite them around to quote. Be specific in telling them exactly what you want.

And don't just accept the first and only quote, as some tradesmen sadly still like to try it on and take advantage of people and give them ridiculous overinflated prices because they think they can get away with it...and you can rant and rave and complain at me all you like saying that doesn't happen - but I can assure you it does!

So get a couple of quotes, and don't book anyone you get a bad gut feeling about, or anyone who annoys you whilst quoting.

For example, patronising, arrogant, unhelpful misogynists who call me 'love' and don't listen are a big no-no for me. You don't have to book, or work with anyone that you don't like.

Plenty more tradesmen in the sea; ones that are lovely and helpful, so we don't need to employ wretches!

Also be aware that the cheapest is not always the greatest.

My electrician is not the cheapest in the area, but that's ok, because he's the best!

It is ok to pay for quality. Sometimes it's false economy to do anything but.

After you've had any skilled trades in to do the work you're not skilled or qualified for, work out the DIY and decorating things you can do yourself.

Obviously doing things yourself is much cheaper in terms of cost, if you can afford the time. YouTube and the internet can be a great help in showing you how to do specific tasks.

But be aware of your own limitations and safety; no silly, dangerous risks, and use adequate personal protective equipment.

If ever in doubt, get a professional in!

Decide what items you want that have to be brand new, non-negotiables – for the rest, a lot of good stuff can be found second-hand on Facebook marketplace.

Be wary when buying anything electrical, but things like furniture, mirrors, decor etc can all be considered - and a lot of time, these things are in good condition and sometimes unopened new surplus items.

For instance, there's masses and masses of internal doors available locally for collection cheaply or free currently, because landlords are having to replace certain ones for fire doors. Doesn't mean the old ones are no good, they're just surplus to that person's requirements!

Shop around for products, don't be scared to use 'trade' firms like Selco, Screwfix, Howdens; they're often not that choosy if you're 'trade' or not.

If you find a particular product you like, get Googling the named product for a better price!

For instance, I spent a few days contemplating a wallpaper called 'Superfresco Glamorous Tweed Charcoal

- I huffed and puffed because it was £18 a roll at the time in Wilkos - but a quick Google showed me it was £12.99 a roll at The Range!

So where do you think I went for it?

And yes, it might only be a fiver difference a roll, but I needed 4-5 rolls – and I'd rather spend that extra £25 on a steak at Miller & Carter!

Decent undercoat is the future on poor or new woodwork before glossing - gloss is dearer, and sits better once on an undercoat paint.

Ditto white matt paint on walls before your expensive colour. It helps your paint hue get the correct colour on the tin. If walls are a bit rough, but not so bad that they need a full plaster, consider a textured wallpaper, then paint a colour on.

Remember we talked about shopping around for the same product?

Paint varies vastly from store to store, even the exact same brand/type, so keep your eyes peeled! Also look out for offers, deals, coupons and such like.

And just gerronwi'it, don't put it off and off once you've got the stuff, as well as being an annoyance, you run the risk of your materials going off or spoiling.

I once put off wallpapering my bay window wall for aaaages after it had been damp-coursed. Then when finally got round to it, I was very annoyed with myself for putting off for so long a small finishing task that literally took me an hour to do.

You'll never finish if you don't start...just gerronwi'it!

So there's a couple of tips to get you started… and don't forget to take 'before and after' photographs so you can see the transformation, and give yourself a pat on the back for your hard work.

Also follow various DIY / project / refurbishment groups for more tips and ideas, as well as inspiration for latest ideas, trends and interior decoration… my favourite at the minute is a Facebook group called **'DIY on a Budget'**.

Good luck, and happy renovating!

FAIR PRICE OR A FLEECING?

CHRISTMAS – WEDDING – NEW YEAR'S EVE – LANDLORD

What do all these words have in common?

I'll tell you: they make the sellers bump up the price of items and services unnecessarily!

You've seen it yourselves in the local shopping centre. A few days before Christmas and shoppers are falling over themselves to buy, in short, utter tat. Christmas presents items such as soap sets, make up, aftershaves, tacky toys, novelty gifts etc.

It's always baffled me why the price of these goods massively increases just because the manufacturers have boxed them up in jazzy snazzy festive boxes aimed for the Christmas market.

Look at the actual products inside, people: you're not telling me it's worth the bumped-up value just because it's in a nice glittery box?!

Ditto New Year's Eve – where many pubs, free for 364 days of the year, now sell you tickets on the door just to let you in to buy their beverages – what's all that about?!

And as for the word 'wedding' – ooof, it's a free reign licence to sting you!
But my gripe today is when contractors bump up the price of a job just because they hear the word LANDLORD.

There is some bizarre assumption by the world as a whole that most landlords are super rich, greedy money-grabbing fatcats.

I am not most landlords.

And although I acknowledge that there are some people in property world exactly like that, in my experience, most of the property landlords I know locally are just hard-working people doing their best to provide a service, and they're not super-wealthy.

Even though we'd like to be!!

But sadly, this urban myth remains prevalent amongst contractors, who persist in giving you ridiculously-prices for services, just because they know you're a landlord.

I have this running joke, when my friends and other people say "Oh, you must be rich, you've got all these houses!"

To which I reply "I'm not rich, BECAUSE I've got all these houses!"

Boilers don't fix themselves you know!

All maintenance and repairs works must be paid for – and sadly the Maintenance Monster rears its head in rental properties way too often for my liking!

Now when I talk about fair prices or fleecing, this is not about me being super tight, or mean, or penny-pinching (oh ok, I am a bit, I'm Yorkshire, but we all are up here!)

I'm not saying that contractors aren't worth their price.

Some definitely are - and they'll know I appreciate their good work and fair fees because I'm loyal; if they look after me, I'll use their services again and again.

Several times recently I have had discussions with contractors, where they were nice guys, I liked them and wanted to give them the business – but then they went and gave me a stupid quote.

And then things get awkward when you have to tell them: 'OWWWW MUCH?!?! That's double what I've ever paid before, sorry, but you're not getting the job.

I know people still need to make a profit, and they've got their own business to run and their own families to feed.

I get that.

But I also know what things are worth, because of my experience and prices I've paid for things before.

Yes, I might be a landlord, but I'm not a gullible moron who wants to set fire to my money just because you're greedy.

So yes, sadly, I do find it difficult to undergo any refurbishment work from fair people for a fair price.

Add into the mix that I'm female and the amount of piss-taking pricing and patronising doubles.

(Don't believe me? Ask any other female property investor!)

I just want a good job done by good guys in a decent timescale for a fair price - without being ripped off – is that too much to ask?!!

It's sheep that follow someone blindly and end up getting fleeced – so you need a fair price, not a fleecing.

Here's a couple of tips when looking for contractors to do work:

1. Find some local firms who provide the service you need. Meeting them in person is good, such as at networking meetings, or ask for referrals from people you know who have used their services.

2. Check them out online, look at their social media, examples of work, testimonials.

3. Arrange for each of your shortlisted contractors to come and do a site visit. Not all at the same time though!

Ps - some of these contractors won't even turn up.

I'm not joking…

If they don't even ring you to explain with a genuine excuse for their absence, remove them from your list.

4. Bear in mind their attitude, personality and demeanour on the site visit.

If you hate them automatically, your gut instinct is giving you a stark warning to avoid avoid avoid!

Like the recent patronising guy who kept calling me 'flower'… Imagine the drama I'd have had getting him to do what I needed without a load of hassle and fuss?!

5. Await quotes. This can be anything from 2 hours to never.

Yes really. Some people you will never hear from again.

I'm still waiting for a quote from a guy from 3 years ago who spent two hours travelling and pricing up a job!

(Makes interesting fun seeing him dance about to avoid me when he attends the same networking meeting…
…hey, maybe he just decided he hates me, and that's ok too!)

6. Assess all the quotes for the best. This might not necessarily be the cheapest.

Stupid quotes can also be removed at this point.

In my head, that's basically the contractor saying: "I don't like you, I don't want to work with you, so I'm going to rip you off". So that's those guys doing you a favour, they've heard the word LANDLORD and those pounds signs starting flashing in their eyes.

Not today, and not with me, my friend!

7. Pick your favourite contractor with their fair quote.

Book them in for the job. Ideally, it's someone you know, like and trust.

8. Let them do the job!

Oversee their work, address any queries that arise, but no need to micromanage or watch over them constantly. They're competent experts, not schoolkid apprentices.

9. I'm going to add this in, as it seems to be a rising problem for contractors…

Once they've done their job to a great standard – pay them!!!

There's been a horrendous rise lately in service providers not being paid for the work they've done, or people withholding their payment for ages - and that's simply not fair.

If they've done you a great job, delivered what you asked, why would you not pay them immediately?

And if you can't afford to do that, then you shouldn't be booking them in for work until you can. *RANT OVER!*

10. Appreciate their efforts. Make sure they know you're thankful for their super work. Leave them online testimonials. Refer them to other people you know. Use their services over and over again.

So there we have it... we all love a fair price, but we hate a fleecing!

And yes, for the record, I am a Libra star sign – the sign of the justice scales, of fairness and equality – so woe betide anyone who tries to upset that balance!

ENERGY?! EPC!!!!!

EEEEEH - PEEEE - CEEEE?!?

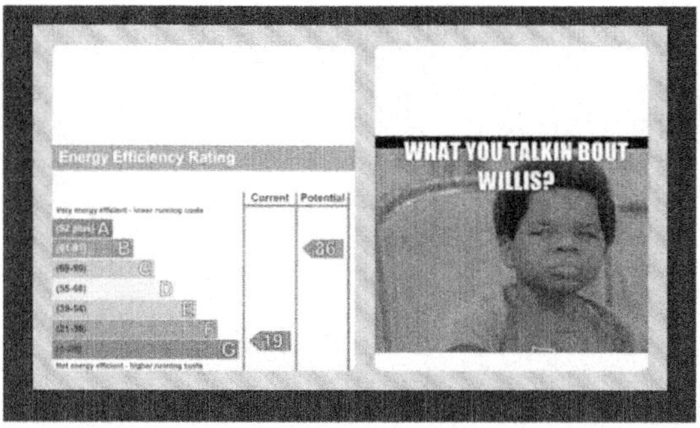

What you talkin' about, Willis?!

Well landlords and property investors, just in case you didn't know about Government legislation with energy efficiency, here is what you need to know! Landlords of privately rented domestic and non-domestic property in England or Wales must ensure that their properties reach at least an Energy Performance Certificate (EPC) of the correct rating before granting a new tenancy to new or existing tenants.

At the time of writing, it's rating E, but that will be going up to rating C imminently. Check the government website for the latest guidelines, rules and legislation.

So if you've bought an old grotbox to do up; a house that hasn't been touched or updated for years, the likelihood is that it won't meet the criteria needed.

This was the case with my recent project; when I bought it, it was rated at Energy Efficiency Rating G, therefore making it illegal to let out.

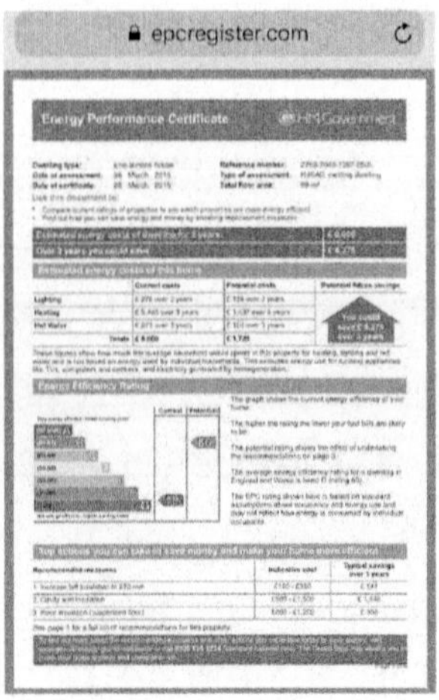
epcregister.com

Energy Performance Certificate HM Government

Now that I've had various works done to it - full rewire and energy efficient lighting, brand new combi boiler and central heating with thermostatic system and heat control valves, amongst a host of other things - it meets the criteria.

But that doesn't matter a jot if your new updated rating isn't listed on the national EPC register! No certificate, no point!

So yes, you've to pay a domestic energy assessor to come out to your house, check what you've changed, and then they'll prepare you a new EPC and put it on the online database.

Here's some insights to help you with improving your energy efficiency ratings:

1.) Know beforehand what the assessor is likely to be looking for, by...

2.) ...acquainting yourself with the www.epcregister.com online. It's free, and you can nosy at the majority of properties in England and Wales by postcode.

3.) Usually there is an old EPC telling you recommendations of what to do to improve the rating. Simply do these within your refurb!

There are a few things to consider which are generally applicable to all properties, the list is here...

Recommended measures
Increase loft insulation to 270 mm
Cavity wall insulation
Floor insulation (suspended floor)
Low energy lighting for all fixed outlets
Change room heaters to condensing boiler
Flue gas heat recovery device in conjunction with boiler
Solar water heating
Solar photovoltaic panels, 2.5 kWp

4.) Once all the works are complete, book your EPC assessor. Many can be found online locally, so shop around.

5.) Make sure your chosen assessor is approved, they should be able to tell you their EES membership number.

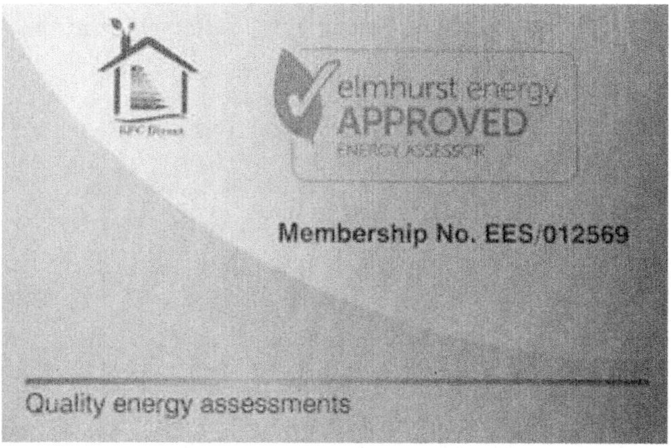

6.) Remember, to legally let out a residential property, the house must be rated as a minimum of the current rating. You will get in bother if they are below this!

Don't panic though, if they are, you are currently still allowed to rent them out, but only on the basis that they started their tenancy before the new rules came into force.

So if you need to upgrade, you can wait until:
a) there's a changeover in tenants and you get new ones
b) your current tenants sign a new tenancy
c) or there's a change in Government policy!

You can't avoid it forever though, and why would you? Sort your houses out so they're legal!

7.) Give your tenants the new Energy Performance Certificate, a tangible paper copy (and get them to sign to say they've received it!), and email a copy to them as well. as evidence of a paper trail audit.

Because if the tenancy all goes horribly wrong, if you haven't given them an EPC beforehand, you won't be able to start the procedure to evict them!

So there we go, a brief overview to being street legal with regards to energy efficiency - Enjoy your energy!!!

IT'S CARPET DAY!!!

Ever since I can remember, I have loved the smell of a new carpet.

Call me weird, but there's something distinctly pleasant about laying down on a new carpet and breathing in its delightful fresh scent.

So you can imagine how excited I get on carpet day – that is, the day of the refurbishment project when the fitter turns up with his vanful of wares – i.e., the carpet you chose the week before.

I readily "roll out the red carpet" for them, and by the way, it really is worth paying extra to have them professionally fitted.

I have tried the DIY carpet fitter role myself, and it just ends up looking like a bodge job. (Don't do it yourself, it's a waste of time, effort, money, stress and carpet)

Bizarrely, no matter how much other refurb work you do in the house, it still always looks unfinished until the floor coverings go down.

This covers up a multitude of sins; mainly old floorboards covered with scruffy paint splashes for the decoration.

So fitting the carpets is pretty much the last stage in the project schedule, meaning the end is nigh; your house renovation is nearly finished!

YEEHAH!!!

But some people get their rug in a twist over what sort of carpet to buy for a rental property. If that's you, don't worry: I wouldn't let anyone pull the rug from under you – *I've got you covered!* (groannn…)

Let me take you on a magic carpet ride to Carpet Choice Kingdom…

<u>Points to consider when choosing a carpet for a rental property:</u>

1. Pick one that's tough and hard wearing. You don't want to be replacing it quite imminently.
2. Make sure it is felt-backed, as it feels softer underfoot.

3. Bleach proof is best, as the inevitable always happens! So it at least gives the tenants a chance at getting their stains out.

4. Pick a neutral colour, but not too light – it hides minor stains.

5. Pick a *pattern* at your peril! They date quite quickly, and often have the effect of making a room look smaller.

6. Underlay, *underlay*?! Arriba!! It depends on your budget and the smoothness of the floorboards underneath, so I don't think it's always a necessity. Make a judgement yourself - and don't let the carpet salesmen walk all over you!

7. Finally, get a pile fabric instead of a loop style carpet. The reason for this is that if a tenant has a pet, if their claws catch on a loop, it snags and rips an entire thread out of the carpet, meaning you're left with a long, unrepairable threadbare snag line.

And that's it!

I'm sure you're not too floored by these revelations, but I hope you hoovered them all up and that these tips help!

PS - Don't be shy about protecting your new carpet – you want your expensive asset to last as long as possible after all.

I have no qualms at asking potential new tenants to remove their shoes on house viewings. If they get stroppy about that, then perhaps they've done you a favour in showing you that they're not the type of respectful tenant you'd want living in your investment anyway!

PPS – I can only apologise for my excessive use of carpet-related puns in this chapter. I'm sure, like an old carpet, you're a little worn out by them, but I'm on a roll; I just can't help myself! I got all these terrible puns from my other carpet-loving friend. Polly Esther.
Definitely it now, take care… and carpet diem!

WHO SURVEYS THE SURVEYORS?

When investing in property, at some point, you will need at some point a property valuation done by a surveyor.

And at some point, everyone in property will have a surveyor who makes an absolutely ridiculous valuation on the property.

Yes, it will happen, and yes, I have had friends who have been told that, for nonsensical reasons, their bought-and-pair for asset has a zero valuation – i.e., the surveyor reckons it's worth nothing, not even the money you paid for it.

Stop laughing / crying – as infuriating and ridiculous as it seems, sadly this does happen!

Despite our best due diligence, our most recent sold and for sale comparables, our best work, time and money spent in refurbishment... there will always be some utter clown of a surveyor who is more interested in covering their own arse than daring to admit what your newly-refurbished property is now actually worth.

What's all that about?!!

Sadly, it's becoming more and more frequent to have a down valuation: I've had it, my friends and all the local investors have had it, so it seems it's a scourge across the board.

Surveyors obviously belong to some evil underground unit, where they get rewarded with down valuation commission. There's no logic to their madness.

What's more infuriating is when the surveyors appear not to even look at the comparables, even when you give them the comparables in their hand.

And what's doubly infuriating is that sometimes you are charged a surveying fee for them to go out and shaft you... #cry

One house I had was EXACTLY the same as the comparable 4 DOORS DOWN, which had sold 7 months earlier. And although mine was NEWLY REFURBISHED, it was EXACTLY the same house, both with internal layout and outside grounds, but the surveyor still valued it LOWER than the twin one twenty metres away.

WHAT'S ALL THAT ABOUT?!?!

If I was if the murderous type, that surveyor would now be under the patio, Brookside style...

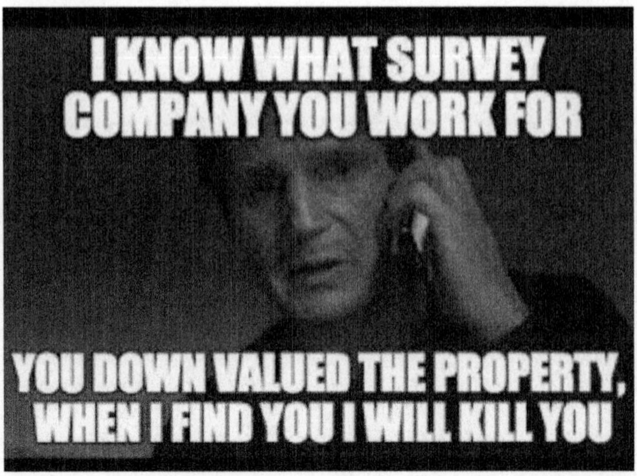

Still, what's the point of my rant?

Well, to help you minimise the risk of this happening, and these are the things you can do to help that.

Minimise the risk when you are doing your due diligence on the property by assuming the end value will be the worst-case scenario. Let's be a pessimist here, then if some miracle happens and they do actually do their job properly, then anything above your worst-case prediction is a Brucie bonus.

Good game, good game!

Look carefully at the comparable properties within a half mile radius in the last two years. And compare apples with apples, for instance a two-bed terrace is not going to be the same as a two-bed semi-detached HOUSE, so find houses that closely match what you have. Look at sold prices, and then current similar properties on the market.

Make a full list of every single refurbishment item you have done in the property. Don't bother putting down what it cost you do each item, it's none of their business! Let them think you've paid more for each item than the savvy tight-fisted bargain-hunting investor you are.

Take clear before and after refurbishment photographs during the project. The grimmer the better! (I mean grim before obviously!)

Stand in each corner of each room and get the shot, then stand in the same places after the refurbishment. Don't forget the exterior and outside space!

Meet the surveyor at the property. Even if it's already tenanted, just explain to your tenant what is going on, and allay their fears that no, there is nothing to panic about, you're not selling the house and they won't end up homeless

Be nice to the surveyor!
Smile!

Make genteel pleasant small talk, and point out things that were absolutely terrible in the house before you had your magic charm fixing them. Confirm the rental amount, with the tenancy agreement if required.

Prepare a little report pack, which you are happy to give to the surveyor. This should include details of the house, your list of refurbishment works, your before and after photos, and some Rightmove screenshots of comparable sold prices and current similar for sale values.

Obviously, make sure you pick some examples which are in realistic keeping with your current property – it's pointless showing them the other ones that sold really cheaply because they needed work!

Pray that your surveyor is not an absolute clown. Keep praying.

If the survey report comes back with a ridiculous valuation, you can either suck it up and take it, change lender (and thus surveyors), or get your mortgage broker to dispute it.

If disputing it, work with your mortgage broker to build up a case of evidence, which politely shows, that actually, Mr Mortgage Surveyor, you're talking tosh, and these are the reasons why.

Another option which may be considered, is to pay for your own independent RICS survey <u>before</u> the mortgage lenders surveyor goes out. This will obviously cost you a couple of hundred pounds, but it makes it more difficult for the surveyor to down value something, when you have placed in their hand a report from the Royal Institute of Chartered Surveyors.

Finally, if all else fails, seek out and destroy the surveyor. There is no other option.

Good luck, and let's hope that the surveyors all get standardised and trained properly very soon!

 # Disclaimer: no surveyors were harmed in the making of my property portfolio.

…but there's always time…

DUDE... WHERE'S MY DEAL??!?

You will get to a point in your property career where you feel that your next property deal eludes you.

You will view lots of houses, put in many offers, but alas, no deal will arise as hoped. This will frustrate you.

You know it's not just any old house you're looking for, because if that was the case, there's hundreds of them locally - but they're all too dear and all too nice.

Where are all the unloved and ropy dumps?

Where's the next grimy little grotbox?

Sometimes there is a real shortage of 'your type' of housing stock at certain times, meaning people will be paying too much for them.

Put your purse away love, it's not even worth that!

Frustration and impatience will kick in - but do we lower our standards and change our criteria?

NO, we do not!

We wait, stealthily, like a panther ready to pounce, for when the "right deal" appears.

We are a master of hard-core discipline, patience and self-control.

We know that our delightful little 2-3 bedroomed scuzzy grotbox, the brick-built house, with no flat roof, with garden for the kiddies, is just around the corner ready to be transformed into a lovely family haven

- and so we shall wait it out… knowing the payoff will be worthwhile.

Meanwhile, for those like me who are occasionally have to sit on their hands…

TOP TIPS FOR THOSE SUFFERING WITH "DUDE, WHERE'S MY DEAL?!?" FEVER

1. I feel your frustration, knowing you've got targets you want to hit. Me too. But if in doubt, wait it out!

2. Have your own criteria of what constitutes a 'deal' to you as a professional property investor, and do not lower your standards. If it's not a deal, then you're just buying a house like Mr & Mrs Normal First-Time-Buyer!

3. Keep yourself detached, and don't get emotional over any one particular property. I too have been guilty of this ("Aww, I used to live on this street") but it's only a house, and unless you're a brick-licking objectophile, then just walk away, Renée!

There's plenty more fish in the sea and bricks in the town!

4. Keep viewing houses and making offers. It's just the Law of Averages. I got three offers bounced last week, but I'll keep smiling about the 'NO's, knowing I'm getting nearer to the 'YES'!

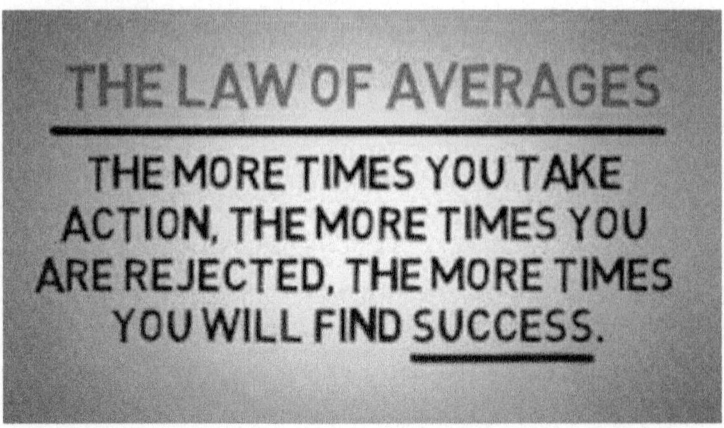

5. Put your bounced offers in a 'pipeline' file. Ring up and check progress with the agents every week, because don't forget, 1 in 3 house sales in the UK falls through.

One of my favourite phone calls goes like this:
"Hello Mr Lovely Estate Agent, how are you getting on with 666 Cantsellit Street? Well let them know my offer still stands if they change their mind!"

And this is repeated weekly, forever, until either it sells (i.e., the purchase exchanges), they accept my offer, or I die.

NB – this really works: for one of my houses, I happened to ring on the very morning a pre-agreed sale had just fallen through - and then I was in there like swimwear!

So keep your chin up, keep smiling, and remember what Mr T says:

YOU JUST HAVEN'T EARNED IT YET, BABY!

In this chapter I'd like to address the rollercoaster ride of building a property business; the frustration and tediousness of "the journey" we're all experiencing.

We all hear everybody's positive stories in life and business and property, and I think it's great to hear them and celebrate their successes along with them.

However, I am baffled by why hardly anybody ever talks about the downsides and negative issues of business development, which is bizarre, because they happen to everyone.

Yet nobody wants to share the disastrous moments, or talk about how they got it wrong, for fear or making us look bad or a failure.

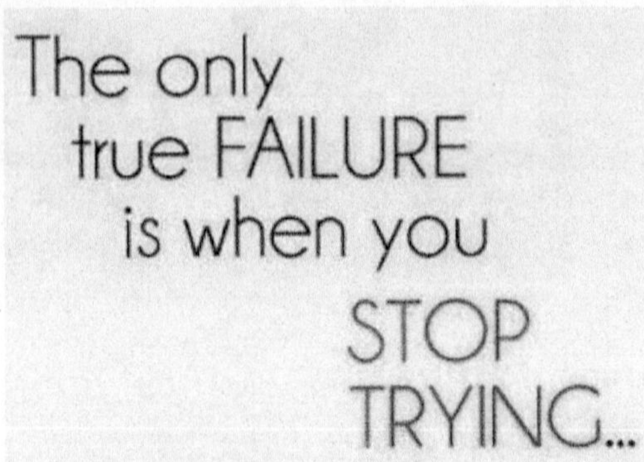

However, I believe we should share our issues, as it comforts other people by showing that we're all in the same boat here, with a couple of evil waves, and guess what: mistakes help us navigate to the good times and sunnier shores!

So in this chapter, I'd really like to help you focus on overcoming adversity, frustration and impatience.

While working hard trying to head towards achieving our targets and goals, I have become aware that things don't always go to plan!

This is very frustrating, as when you spend a lot of your time and energy (and money!) actually putting things into place to make them happen, it can be infuriating when your goals remain out of reach.

Why is this? For all of you Smith's fans out there, I refer to one of their finest yet lesser-known pieces of work, the song in which Morrissey claims "You Just Haven't Earned It Yet, Baby"

If you've not heard this particular song, you'll enjoy listening to Johnny Marr's jangling guitar and Morrissey's oscillating catchy melody. Why is it such a good song? "I'll tell you why-y-y-y-y…."

Google it immediately, you'll get the gist of what I mean!

I'll let you into a little secret, when I feel horrendously miserable and desperately need to cheer myself up, I listen to this superb song from 1987 as (surprisingly for a Smiths' song!) it always has the effect of lifting my mood.

In fact, if you feel just like Morrissey, who quotes:

"If you're wondering why, when all I wanted from life was to be famous, I've have tried for so long, it's all gone wrong…"

Then let's address that…

Everyone has bad days - even the poor guy you saw this morning whose top-of-the-range Audi had broken down in the middle of the motorway.

My friends chuckle about my mentality, because they say I am a very black-and-white, no-nonsense person.

There is no in-between for me.

There is no grey area.
Things either go really well for me, or else the world is falling in.

Or as Morrissey tells me: “You must suffer and cry for a longer time”

Many times throughout my property career I have felt like banging my head against the wall, simply because things haven't gone my way.

Many times I have wanted to cry, but we don't do such things where I’m from, because if you do, your mum says "Stop crying or I’ll gi’ ye someat to cry about!"

So we just toughen up, pull up our big girl pants and get on with it.

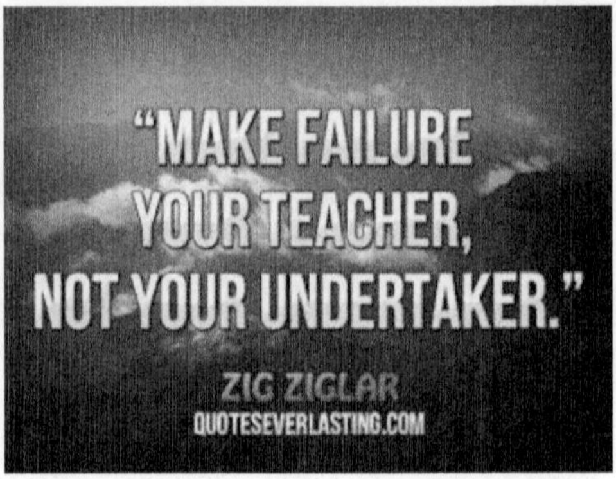

Why have all these disasters not made me just give up and walk away with my tail between my legs? Quite simply, persistence and pure stubbornness.

I'm too stubborn to let this beat me!

When you're going through hell, just keep going.

Winners never quit, because quitters never win.

One thing that has helped though is the system of writing down reasons why you are doing this.
I have written down a list of “50 reasons stating why I will make this succeed”. These are reasons such as “So I don’t have to work for my boss”, or “So I have more time to spend with my family” or “So I can afford to take my mum on a nice trip”, or “So I can finally enjoy my success and be proud of my achievements”. And so on…

Give this a go, this list will see you through tough times, when everything feels like it’s going wrong and you want to give up.

Everybody talks about the ‘big why’ but when you have sat down and thought about lots and lots of little whys, then it becomes clear to you that you really don't need to sweat the small stuff.

In a few years' time, when all has gone well, no doubt you will look back and laugh at the time when things went wrong.
Another tactic I use to help when things go wrong is allowing myself five minutes to have a little tantrum and get all my frustration out.

I remember one particular time I ranted and raved about how someone I had contracted had turned out to be incompetent - and after several minutes of venting, my mother nodded and smirked and said "Have you quite finished now?!"

And I had.

The final way I have of coping with catastrophes is my little phrase that "Things are always better after a sleep".

So if you are really so incredibly frustrated, take yourself off for a little nap - and magically on awakening, things are not as bad as they first seemed.

Alongside that, I enjoyed reading 'The Compound Effect' book by Darren Hardy. Just because you're working hard now and not seeing results, it doesn't mean they won't materialise in the near future. Keep going – you just haven't earned it yet baby!

Even the worst day is only 24 hours, so tomorrow is a fresh start.

So to summarise:

Top Tips for overcoming frustration, impatience and adversity

1. Listen to the song "You Just Haven't Earned It Yet, Baby"

2. Fill-in your list of 50 reasons why you must succeed

3. Vent when things go wrong. A problem shared, and all that!

4. Things are always better after a sleep

5. Read 'The Compound Effect' book. All good things come to those who wait…and work hard continuously!

#BONUS#

Have a think about everything that has gone right in both your journey and life so far.

See, it's not so bad, is it? Look at everything you've been through, and yet here you are, still, wanting to do great things.

Well done you! You're doing better than you think you are, so don't be so hard on yourself!

Only losers quit, and we are destined to be winners if we don't give up.

Remember, you will never beat anyone who refuses to give up.

WHEN OVERWHELM GETS OVERWHELMING

Ever bitten off more than you can chew?

I've been there, and I know exactly how I felt.

One particular project I finally got the keys to the house I had purchased after a lengthy conveyancing period, and on entering the property, I remembered and reflected on all the work it needed, which could only be described as a bombsite – and I had a little panic.

I knew, in the future, once it was done, it would be good; a lovely family home for rental.
But that was in the future; not the overwhelming moment I was standing in right now.

And as I stood in this bombsite house which required immense rectification, realising the enormity of the task before me, I knew I had bitten off more than I could chew.

So I will freely admit I felt overwhelmed.

I had refurbished houses before this point, even a large vastly-outdated one, and a scruffy repossession. But at the time, this one surpassed anything I'd done before, as it was by far the worst house I'd had.

However, the condition of the house was nothing compared to the continuous overwhelming thought I had:

"My mum's going to do her nut when she sees the state of this"

The next day I took my beloved mother to see this house.

In the early days of my property career, when funds were tight, a lot of the refurbishment works come from my own fair hands.

Or more accurately, my mummy's - what with me being pretty pathetic at manual labour, as well as accident-prone, and to be blunt, uselessly gormless.

So knowing that poor mummy will be involved in this wreck, I dreaded her crossing the threshold.

Normally on viewings when the houses are terrible, she is very vocal in telling me how terrible they are. On that day as she stood in my new bombsite wreck, even she was overwhelmed into silence.

I suspect had she been with me when viewing this one, her comments would undoubtedly have been the usual: "Don't bloody get this one, it's a right tip, I'm not doing this one, look at the state of that kitchen, clatty cow, and it stinks of cat piss...etc etc".

But that day she realised it was too late: I'd bought it, and we were committed to this house.

And her stunned silence made me think: bloody hell, what have I done??

And then I told her we had a ridiculously low budget because the solicitors' completion bill had been horrific - and that we had to turn it around in twelve weeks.

She gave me a look that made me think I was getting murdered right there and then.

It was horrendously overwhelming.

A fleeting thought occurred; that maybe we weren't up to it.

Maybe I had taken too much on.

Maybe I'm not ready for such a big project.

Maybe I'm just not cut out to do this.

But it was tough sh!t now.
The decision had been made: there was only one way, and it's forward.

And as we stood there, in this absolute bombsite, two resilient Leeds lasses, with hard lives behind us, we realised we would have to toughen up and "gerronwi'it" – just like we always have.

So I came home, and decided to rationalise, self-soothe, concoct a cunning plan - and have a word with mysen.

And if this chapter recalling this incident helps someone else new in property who is also feeling overwhelmed, then that is a bonus.

Thus…

Overcoming Overwhelm - Kellyann's Top Tips:

Remember that a journey of a thousand miles starts with a single step. So take a deep breath, and move forward. We will get there in the end, but we must keep moving. Standing still is stagnation. And failure is not an option!

Next: how do you eat an elephant? Break it into chunks!

Assess the works needed in each room. List them down. Work out the order each item must be done in.

Use online refurbishment planners to help.

Collate your contractors. Use the superb professionals you've used before, or had recommended locally. Get them telephoned and booked in to visit the site for quotes.

Become the professional you need to be in order to succeed. I will need to evolve to become a top project manager extraordinaire.

What a chance to learn new skills!

Be like Winston Churchill: despite suffering depression, he once said "I am an optimist. It does not seem much use being anything else."

So think of the positives. For instance: the house is roomy, dry, secure, clean(ish), with a massive garden, and will be a superb rental - and will provide another family with a long-term home.

Finally, give yourself a talking to. Have a word with yoursen. Pull your big girl/boy/other pants up, dry your eyes and get on with it.

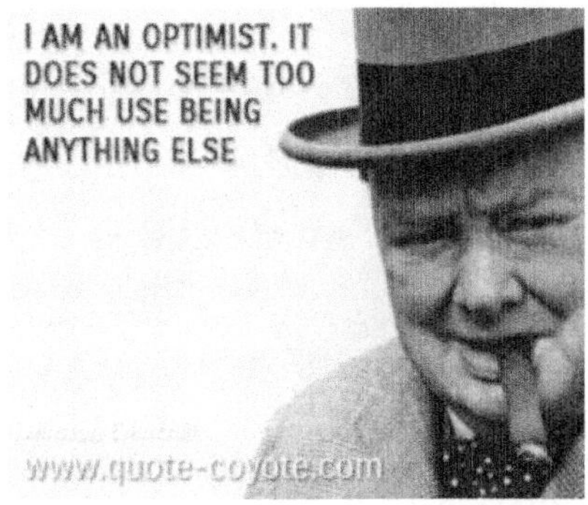

Nothing is impossible, but if you do nothing, nothing will happen. It's said that the distance between your dream and reality is called your action.

My little imaginary rental family couldn't move in until I've made it safe and habitable for them.
So best get cracking!

(NB – I did get this overwhelming project finished, my imaginary family became a real one, and they've lived there happily for five years now – keep the end in mind when you're pushing through your comfort zone!)

Remember, if being in property was that easy, everyone would do it. But there is no competition, because nobody else is you. And we're going to make this work.

So you can bugger off ***Overwhelm***; there's no room for you in the works schedule!

Because, in terms of progress and success: what's the point in coming this far to *only* come this far?!

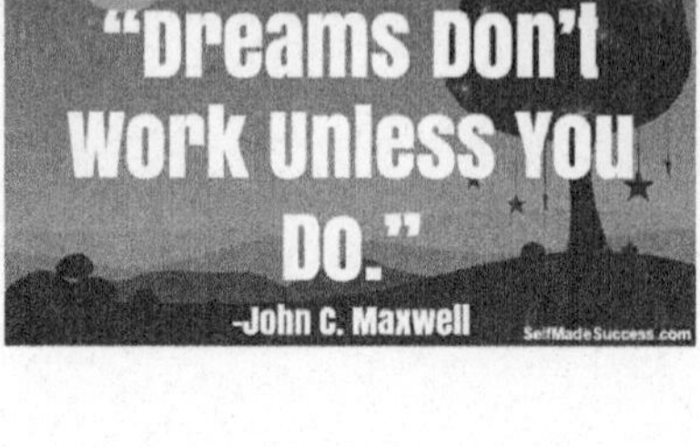

TANTRUM TIME: WHAT TO DO WHEN THINGS GO WRONG

Listen, I'm not going to sugar-coat it for you: lots of things go wrong in property. Often.

Endlessly, sometimes.
You've got be a very resilient, stubborn and strong-minded creature to be in the business - either naturally be that personality, or grow into that mindset.

Because if you don't, you will end up a sad, miserable, nervous wreck rocking in a corner, crying your eyes out most days. I revisit my previous chapter's teaching: property really isn't for everybody!

Here's a lesson I learned early on when something went badly wrong, and I wrote the piece which constitutes this next part of the chapter as an attempt to self-soothe.

I was INFURIATED as I wrote these next paragraphs some years ago, but as I wrote, I felt better relaying into print this hapless tale of disappointment.

This was what happened…

All week I had been looking forward to my coaching session at 1pm near Birmingham with a business coach.

I had prepped my materials, thought about my vision, planned the journey with handwritten directions

(I'm old-school), and even ironed a shirt! (ironing is the work of the devil, so not common in mein haus)

I knew it would take me 2 hours 4 minutes to drive the 120.6 miles, so I left my house at 10:17am, with 2 hours and 43 minutes to do it in, you know, just in case things went wrong.

And then I got in my car... and the piece of sh!t wouldn't start.

I don't give up that easily though, so tried many dozen times to get it going, encouraged it with various colourful names, and rang two manly men for advice and assistance - to no avail.

Then I thought I would try and push it backwards down my drive to try and bump-start it - only to smash the hanging basket planter off the wall with my car door.

Then I got really desperate and went and asked my elderly pensioner neighbour if he could help. He tried, bless him, but couldn't, mainly because my drive is uphill, tight and narrow, with no chance of using another car to jump start it.

I am, in the words of Colonel Abrams, Trapped, like a fool, I'm in a cage, I can't get out…

Now I'm sure you've been there yourself, and experienced that overwhelming frustration and downright infuriation about things you've planned going wrong because of external causes.

What I hate most of all in situations like this is the utter sense of hopelessness. You've exhausted all other options, and it is exasperating that still you can't do anything to make it right in the timeframe.

So as I sit here and wait for Green Flag to come and do some manly mechanical magic, I contemplate how to cheer myself up from my bitter disappointment.

I read a top tip yesterday in Jen Sincero's book 'You Are A Badass' that said when bad things happen, you should turn it around by starting with 'I'm glad this happened because...'

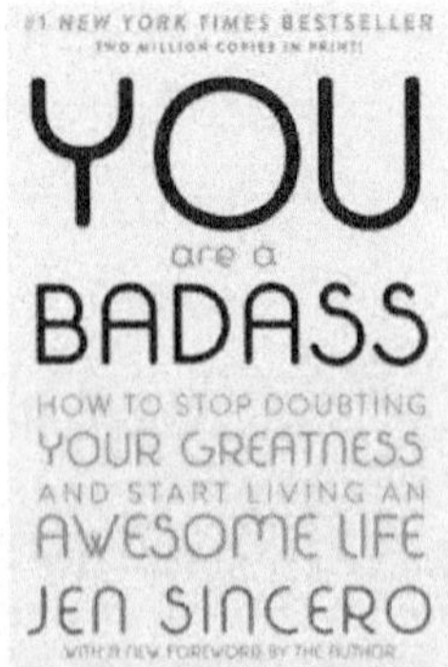

So here goes:
I'm glad my car broke down because…

- gosh this is hard, I'm not glad at all… no, keep going…

- it's a warning that something is not quite right with my car, which could have led to something more dangerous.
- it's a lesson that life occasionally gets in the way of plans.
- it's shown to me that I at least try to be reactive and resourceful in times of need.
- it proves that bad things happen to everyone at times, through no fault of their own.
- it's made me grateful of every single other time that the car didn't let me down.

- it's made me realise that I can't have my own way all the time
- it's shown me that having a shouting, swearing tantrum has absolutely no effect, other than putting myself in a bad mood. So therefore it's pointless wasting energy doing it in future.
- it helps me put problems into perspective.

Nobody died, and only death is unfixable. So get a grip of yourself.

Feel a bit better now, after I've had a word with myself.

I'm glad I read that top tip yesterday… because it's helped today when things went wrong.

And thus, I hope passing on this tip helps you avoid a tantrum when things go wrong.

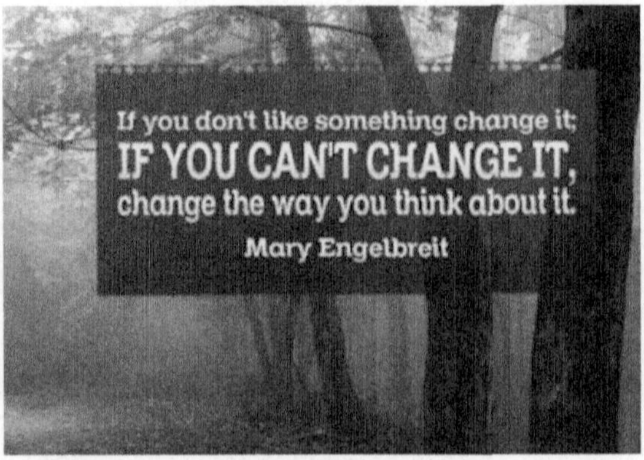

So that's the piece of text I wrote at the time all those years ago.
The advice still stands.
It helped then, and it still helps now.

NOW LISTEN...
Ladies and gentlemen, when writing those last few paragraphs at the time, I was feeling so utterly frustrated, disappointed and angry.

But let me tell you this, on reflection, some years later: it is clear that sometimes the universe works in very mysterious ways, ways which we don't always understand at the time.

Since that day, when my car unexpectedly refused to behave itself, that particular car didn't let me down in that way again. It has never since refused to start, either before or after that day.

Here's what transpired…

…Because I didn't get to go that day, despite my explanation and apologies to said business coach guru, they never gave me a new meeting date. I never got to another chance to go meet them again.

And although I was frustrated at the time, in hindsight, that was a lucky escape - knowing what I know now, years later, and knowing the events that turned out...
Because that 'business coach guru' turned out to be a massive con artist.

Full of bluff and blunder and rented possessions, cars, properties, watches etc to make themselves look more impressive and successful than they really were.

They defrauded many, many people out of tens of thousands of pounds, with their supposed integrity and 'hard work' - all built upon a house of cards, with smoke and mirrors, and clever marketing.

I know someone who fell for their charms, and parted with a lot of money, to end up with nothing. A lovely guy, utterly duped and betrayed and let down and ripped off, totally unfairly.

That could have been me.

That could also be you, if you're not careful in checking out the people you work with - so there's another key lesson in undertaking proper due diligence on everybody you choose to do business with.

But back to the original point: sometimes when you feel things go wrong, it's because the universe works in mysterious ways, and perhaps has a better plan for you.

Because how bizarre, that on the one day I was due to meet with a business fraudster, my reliable trusty car just outright refused to move.

Weird, eh?!

Things do go wrong, and often these things can be fixed… but sometimes they are simply blessings in disguise.

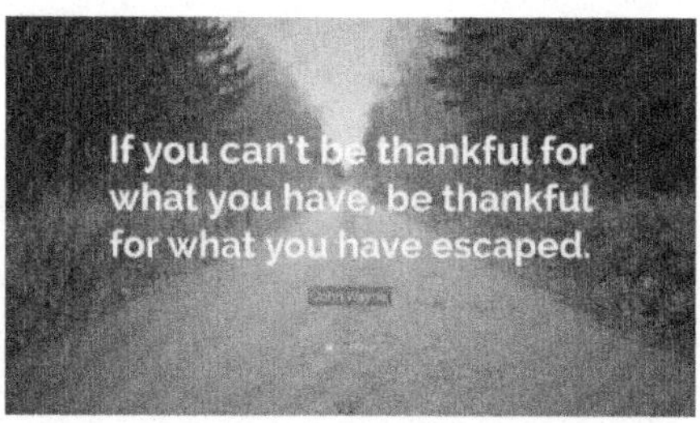

WORRIES AND CONCERNS OF PRIVATE INVESTORS

In this chapter we'll start to look at working with private investors, also known as angel investors.

These are people who agree to invest in opportunities for a greater return on their capital, such as a property deal, and I will be addressing common worries of investors:

If you were an angel investor, with spare money to invest, what sorts of things would you be worried or concerned about when looking to invest in a deal?

Here are a couple of common worries and concerns:

Investor Concern: Money sat in the bank earning very little!

At the time of writing, research shows the best interest rates right now... with the top earner being just 1.11% APR - ANNUAL PERCENTAGE YIELD!!! That means if you have £20,000, your interest PER YEAR is only like to be around £222... yes it's alright, but it's nothing to get that excited about.

Especially when you take into account the current UK inflation rate...

A better way to grow your wealth is to invest it.

Say for example, into a hands-free passive property deal, where your return on investment will be much higher than any current UK bank interest rates.

Property really does enable us to beat the banks!

Investor Concern: No time or knowledge to invest funds

Whilst it's important that you have an overview of how the investment process works, it's not always necessary that you know everything about property: the area, the strategy, the tenant type, the project type, the refurbishment works, and the refinance process.

Add to that that you may not physically have time to research all the above - nor the inclination!

It is quite acceptable, and actually very common to be an armchair investor.

That means you are someone who invests passively, with as a hands-free option i.e., you don't get directly involved in the project's happenings day-to-day.

You just invest, then sit back and watch the big picture unfold, knowing the project is working to build your wealth.

So no, you don't have to be a property expert in order to invest in property.
You just have to find someone who is!!

Investor Concern: How secure and safe is their money?

This is a common concern for people, because with the volatility of other investment methods, you want to be sure that you will get your money back.

Stocks and shares go up and down in value, and you may end up losing money.

Ditto with cryptocurrency and trading.

Banks are relatively safe with your funds (assuming they don't go bust!), but your interest rate is poor.

Property is safe because it is a tangible asset, built of bricks and mortar. It really exists - so should the worst happen, such as the developer unexpectedly dying during the project (cheery!), at least the investor will still be able to sell off the property to recoup their funds.

Not only that, property consistently increases in value over time, meaning your money really is secure within a property deal.

Ever heard the term "safe as houses"?!

That applies to your property investment too!

Investor Concern: Not knowing who to trust with their money.

This is without a doubt the most important part of any investment.

Anyone can say anything to anybody in order to extort money from them.

Don't let yourself be fooled and taken for granted by people who do not have the best of intentions for you.

If you are investing finance with someone for a property project, please ensure they are confident and competent at bringing to the project:

- **knowledge**
- **skills**
- **education**
- **experience**
- **network**
- **power team**
- **problem solving**
- **focus**
- **time**
- **energy**
- **honesty**
- **integrity**

If you're not sure that they can provide all this, then walk away from the deal!

PRIVATE INVESTORS… WHAT'S IN IT FOR THEM?

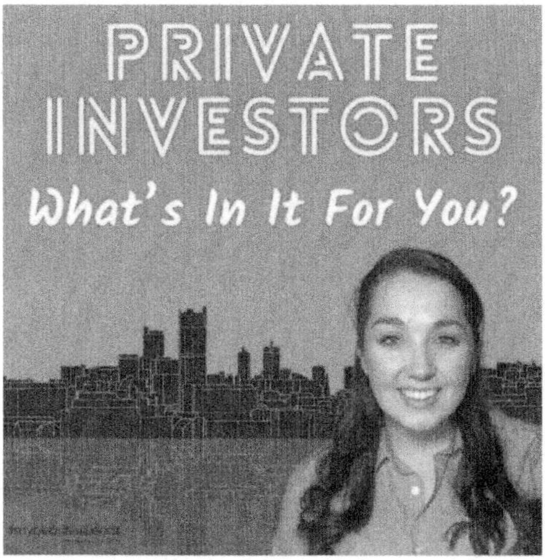

You might already know that I help people build wealth passively, through the vehicle of property.

They lend me money for a property project, I do the project, they get a great return whilst I do all the work, I retain the residential property and rent it out to a lovely local family.

But have you ever wondered why people invest?

Why would people with funds want to work with me?

Or indeed why would they want to invest with you?

In this chapter I'll be exploring the reasons of what's in it for them as private investors.

Because let me be blunt here: property costs money.

And sometimes if you haven't got enough funds for your plan, you need to leverage other people's money to make your vision happen.

That's how investment works for all business opportunities.

First of all, a key reason people choose to invest is that it gives them somewhere **safe** to invest their funds.

They realise that property is a good solid asset, and is unlikely to be stolen or magically disappear or reduce in value, like stocks, shares and other volatile online investment vehicles.

Property is a safe investment option, because it's a tangible asset which really exists.

That's why we have the phrase **"Safe as Houses"**!

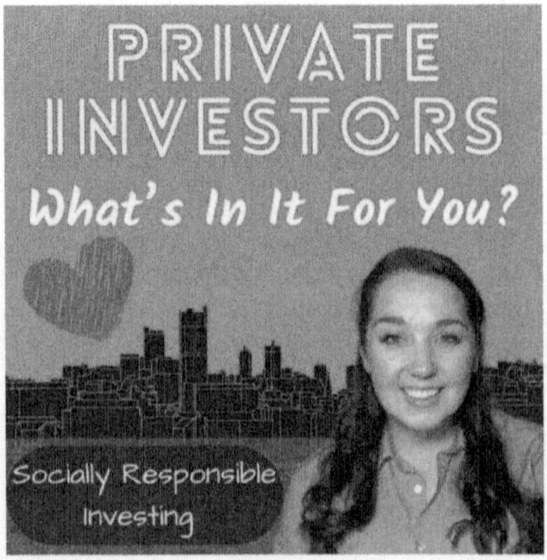

Another great reason people choose to work with me is that they know it involves **socially responsible investing.**

They're not putting their money into dubious activities, products or gambling - they are directly benefitting local families by providing housing.

There's nothing more socially responsible than helping low-income families get a safe, secure home to comfortably bring their kids up in.

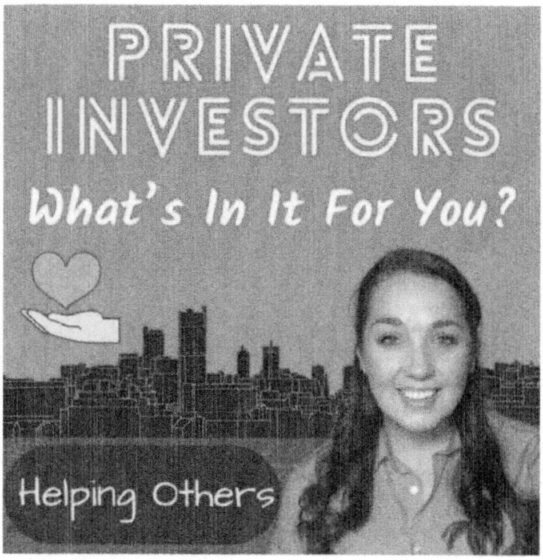

Here's another key reason that I know many people want to invest with me: **it gives them the chance to help me help others.**

Not only does it help provide housing for people, it helps me build my own future, and it helps them build their own wealth!

It's nice to be nice, it gives you a good feeling inside. It is often said that we rise by lifting others, and that helping others is the secret sauce to a happy life.

I fully believe this; in fact, I even wrote a **blog** on the subject - do have a read!

It's called 'The Benefits of Helping Others', and can be found on my website.

https://kellyannmartin.co.uk/2019/02/26/the-benefits-of-helping-others/

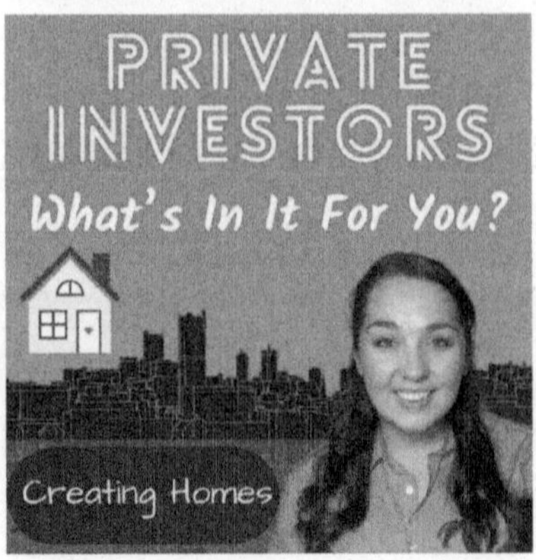

At present in Britain, there is a severe housing shortage.

Every year we need an extra 300,000 homes in addition to the new ones that have been built, just to keep up with demand.

Investing with me, or a similar property developer, gives investors the knowledge that they're helping create much-needed homes.

Demand vastly outstrips supply, which means your investment funds are providing a much-needed commodity.

There'll always be a need for housing, meaning there'll always be investment required to fund this - meaning you will be financially rewarded for the value you provide through investment funding.

Finally, a good draw for private investors is that they have the opportunity to make far more interest on their funds than they would by having it sat in the bank.

If you have £20,000 idly sitting in your high street bank, at current Bank of England interest rates, you are only likely to make around 25p interest per month.

Whereas if you put that £20,000 into one of my property projects, **you are guaranteed a minimum of 6% per annum**, which means you would receive £1200 interest per annum - which equals £100 a month in interest!

That's a much better return than 25 pence, isn't it?!?

How can I afford to give you such a high return?

Well, that's because of the magic of uplifting the values of property development.

There's always enough money in the deal to enable me to do this, and investors deserve a great return for their trust in me and helping me deliver these projects.

Win-win for all!

Investors help me provide housing, and I help them grow their wealth passively within short periods of time.

It's a great feeling to give someone back a large chunk of money in interest, knowing you have effectively beaten the banks!

So there we have it: a range of reasons explored as to what's in it for private investors who choose to invest in my property project opportunities.

LISTEN PEOPLE: **<u>you can do this too.</u>**

There's no magic about me. I just do what I say I'm going to do.

Follow the system, have a great plan and a great property deal, find some investors, make the investment a win-win scenario, don't let them down, and don't be a wretch.

Once you've shown great integrity with them on one deal, they're likely going to want to work with you again.

Integrity is key.

THE CREDIBILITY OF PEOPLE YOU'RE INVESTING WITH

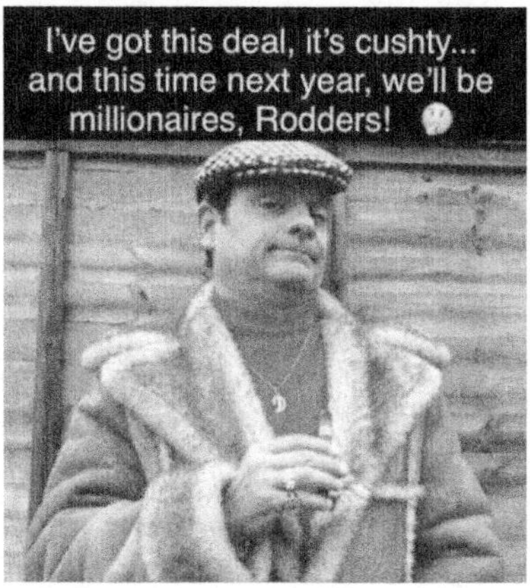

I love property, but sadly the property investment industry is rife with sharks and peddlers, out to separate you from your hard-earned funds.

Most people active in property know of many other property people across the country.

Now that social media is a key part of business, it's very easy to see what other people in the industry are doing – and how they are behaving…

Here are a couple of examples of investment horror stories.
Obviously, it wouldn't be fair to name them, but I suspect other property people will know of them.

A development guru who promised big things with investors' funds; took lots of finance from people for large projects, and then disappeared into oblivion – absconded from the UK, now living abroad.

A property training provider who delighted in showing off an expensive cars and trips and living in the lap of luxury, all the while having not paid back hundreds of thousands of pounds to investors they owed money to.

A charismatic and seemingly successful developer – having made a series of choices and mistakes leading to debt and disaster and personal crises, which ultimately led to their downfall.

So with all these sharks infesting the waters with their seeming greed and lack of morals and ethics, the key question here is, before you invest your money with them: **what do you really know about them, and their knowledge, experience and credibility?**

And most importantly: their **integrity** as a person?

Thank God evil, devious, and greedy Mr Burns is just a cartoon character!

Here's a couple of ways in which you can check out the credibility of someone you're considering investing with:

Watch them. And not just for a short while; for months and months, or longer if necessary. As long as it takes for you to feel comfortable that they are who they say they are. Meet them in person, if possible, several times.

Stalk them from afar. I fully expect that anyone considering me will have checked me out in the ways I'm about to suggest. I encourage it.

And that's absolutely fine, because if you've nothing to hide, you've nothing to worry about.

Does what they say and do seem **real**? Can they **prove it**? It's all very well them saying they've done this, that and the other, but **where's their evidence**? They should be able to show you case studies, legal documents, Land Registry certificates and so on. I am happy to showcase any of my projects, and always ask if anyone wants to visit – obviously that's easier to do during the refurbishment stage when there's no tenants living there to pester!

Companies House should show you a few things about them – but remember it doesn't show you everything, and it's not always fully up to date. For instance, it shows you the properties I have within my limited company, but it doesn't show the ones in my personal name. If in doubt, or if something doesn't tally up with what they're saying – just ask them!

Their **credit file score and credit report** – are they willing to show you it? Be aware of missed payments, unserviced debts built up, county court judgments and so on. It is best when they have lots of ticks every single month, and a nice high score. And if there is some minor blip, can they explain it? For instance, credit card balances might be down to buying a new boiler, not just simply a bad spending habit on shoes and handbags!

The deal they are offering: does it actually stack up? Can you see exactly how and when your money will be returned? Is it realistic? **Openness and honesty** is key here. Last year I had to tell an investor that the deal simply couldn't afford to give them the interest rate that they were looking for – there wouldn't be enough in it within the deal to make it viable. What's the point in making fake promises you can't deliver on? No point – so make sure you ask lots of questions, even the awkward ones.

Recommendations, referrals and testimonials.

Now in the work I do, it's easy to get feedback about my property and tenancy work – but not so easy to get angel investor testimonials. Why? Well put quite simply, it's not really fair to ask someone who has invested with you to publicly admit to the world that they've lent you money – even though you did a good job and returned it in full and on time with the agreed rate!

We're still a little shy in the UK about talking about our money, and I fully respect that my investors probably won't want other people harassing them to lend them funds. However… do they have people willing to tell you about their **personality and character**? The length of time they've known that person, and in what capacity? The work they've seen from them? Dig dig dig for that information, especially if you've not known them very long!

I hope all this helps you, no matter who you choose to make an investment with. **If you don't know, like and trust someone, you definitely shouldn't be working with them.**

It's vitally important that you protect your assets at all costs, and you've every right to be suspicious and cautious – in fact I strongly encourage you to be!

Because it's very likely that you've worked hard for your funds – so don't let some wretch disappear with them.

And as new property investors/ developers, now you've had an insight into what kinds of due diligence angel investors go through to select people they work with.

So if you can provide all the aforementioned items, do the right thing, get your evidence in order, you won't go far wrong.

HOW DO YOU KNOW WHO TO TRUST WITH YOUR MONEY?

I'm including this chapter because of a little occurrence that happened, which I wasn't able to stop thinking about.

I had put my car in for the MOT in the morning and so had to get the bus into Leeds. I was booked in to attend a workshop.

Whilst I was on the bus, it went through one of my property investment patches, one of the poorer areas.

A young lass on the seat behind me began having a phone conversation. Now I didn't have much choice but to listen to this girl's conversation, and as it panned out, I began to feel sorry for her.

She was on the phone to what appeared to be some sort of loan or debt repayment company - explaining how she was baffled that a payment of £19 had been missed and that she couldn't afford the double payments of £38 plus a £12 late payment charge.

I listened, and felt bad for her - especially as during her conversation she triggered all my emotional key phrases, such as "I'm a single mum", "I can't afford that", and "If I pay you all that I'm going to be left short this week".

This phone call had lasted ten minutes by now while she argued her case.

I had a discreet look round at her, bearing in mind I hadn't seen her up to now, just heard her phone call.

She was a young lass in her early 20s, plainly and casually dressed. She looked quite tidy, not rough or drug-addicted, nor too extravagant, jazzy or flashy - just a normal young girl who appeared to be having some hardship.

I ummed and aahed to myself, and decided that I would try and help her.

I looked in my purse. I'm a bit like the Queen these days in that I don't often carry real money anymore (in fact did you know that only 30% of transactions in the UK now are cash? But that's another story…)

However, I had a £5 pound note in my purse.

It wasn't much, but it would make me feel better knowing that she'd have enough cash to make sure she had food for her kid.

I thought about my plan to give her this fiver.

What if she was insulted?

Humiliated?

In the past, I've had people feel sorry for me, when I was a skint kid with a poor single mother - and I know how that humiliation burns.

Her conversation continued, and she mentioned to the person on the other end of the line that she was annoyed that she was having to have this embarrassing conversation on a public bus.

I felt her humiliation for her, the last thing anyone wants to be doing is airing private problems in front of everyone.

The bus arrived at the main stop on Leeds and everyone started to disembark. She got up, continuing her phone call, and I immediately got up after her, discreetly touched her on the arm and tried to give her the fiver.

What happened next baffled, confused and surprised me.

She laughed, moved the phone away from her face and said, “Oh it’s alright, don’t worry, I’m lying to them”. And then a farcical scenario occurred, where I didn’t believe her, tried to give her the money anyway and she laughed and refused.

I got off the bus absolutely bewildered.

I contemplated this.

I thought how convincing her story was.

How plausible.

And how I, normally cynical and savvy, had believed what I had heard from her. Am I going soft?

How could I have not spotted that she wasn't genuine?

I'm normally so good at spotting fibs and incongruencies; my gut instincts are very strong.
And then I was baffled: she had easily lied to a stranger on the phone that she didn't know, but then told the truth to someone right in front of her, when they offered the help of money.

I laughed at this juxtaposition.

Was she lying to them?

Or just lying to me?

And if them; are things really so bad that being short of £19 is an issue?

What would have happened if I'd had a twenty-pound note to offer?

I genuinely thought that she needed help, and tried to give her it.

We don't see people as they are, but as we are.

What would you have done in that situation?

And how would you have reacted to her revelation?

I went on to my workshop, which was about private investment.

It became absolutely clear to me that you really need to know someone very well when making an investment.

How can you ever be sure you trust someone with your money?

And know for certain that they're not a wretch?

I've met people before, and within half an hour of meeting them, they've offered to lend me money. This makes me very nervous and dubious, and I tell them, "But you hardly know me!".

It makes me concerned how easily other people agree to things so quickly. I'm nervous for them: not because I'm a wretch who will rip them off – but because there are other people out there who will.

I want people to know me first before they invest with me.

Because although I know that I'm trustworthy, it's very important to me that I know that other people know that I am trustworthy as well.

I'm not content with just taking someone's money to invest if I think they're uneasy about me.

After all, anyone could say anything on the internet, and perhaps, like me, you could be fooled by a one-sided conversation.

My point is this: meet people in person before investing anything: time, effort, or money.

Get to know them.

Watch what they do and how they behave, over a period of time.

Get proof that they are what they say they are.

Because I would absolutely hate to think that someone has taken advantage of your good nature.

Even if it is only a fiver...

The five-pound note in question!

Remember this story as a property developer looking for investment.
It is a big deal for someone to have that much trust in you that they will lend you vast amounts of money for your property projects.

Respect that trust, by always doing the right thing.

Always.

PROPERTY MISTAKES I WON'T BE REPEATING

In my career as property developer, I've made some mistakes.

Mistakes cost you time, effort, stress, and money. We want to preserve our sanity at all costs!

It's good not to make mistakes to start with, or even better, learn from other people's mistakes!

Here's a selection of my biggest howlers over the years... laugh along with me... but don't repeat these daft mistakes yourself!

One big boo-boo I won't be repeating: putting laminate floor in rental houses!

I had it in my own house for a while, it was trashed after just 18 months so I took it out... so why did I think it would be hardwearing enough for tenants?!

The one rental house I put it in, their pets kindly seeped that laminate in urine… lovely

So into the tip that lot went when they left, a mistake never to be repeated!

Here's another property mistake I won't ever be repeating: asking for investment funding on too short a timescale!

A lovely investor offered to lend me money for a project, but I only asked for 2 months to bridge a gap before my refinance money came through - which in hindsight was ridiculous on my part.

What happened next was that my planned project got gazumped, and I couldn't get another property acquired fast enough and time ran out.

But because I always do as I've promised I then gave the investor their money back plus their couple of grand interest as agreed - despite not even ending up with a project!

But… that same investor, having seen I can be trusted, went on to lend me funds for two other projects.

And although it was an expensive lesson for me, I now know to always ask for at least a 12-month investment period for projects, just in case something goes wrong!

Hey ho, we live and learn from our mistakes - we just don't do them again!!!

Another mistake I've made was not creating enough storage.

This wasn't apparent at the beginning, where the kitchen units were adequate for a single mum. My logic for not adding more was they might want to use that wall and space for a dining table.

But fast forward a couple of years, and the family of 2 had grown to a family of 6, and they were struggling for storage space.

There is never enough storage, even in my own house, so we added these additional six units to the kitchen to relief the storage burden.

Good learning for the future!

I'll tell you another property mistake lesson I learnt the hard way - not inspecting enough!

In one of my early rentals, the family just had a baby, seemed nice, so I mostly left them to it.

Fast forward 3 years when they moved areas, the entire house and floor coverings stunk and were ruined by the fact the tenants had accumulated SIX dogs!

Bear in mind, their letting agency tenancy agreement stated no pets allowed, so the agency obviously hadn't been inspecting either… it was the neighbour afterwards who told me about their illegal half dozen dog collection!

So there you go, keep inspecting your property on a regular basis!

Oh gawwwd, another property mistake not to be repeated… dodgy decor colours!

Now bear in mind I am no interior designer…

My first few houses all had what I call 'The BMW Treatment' - Beige Magnolia White!

That was when magnolia boxes were the "in thing"!

Then I got a load of cheap paint - about 40 tins of the stuff - which was used in the next couple of houses (hey, we're always on a budget!)

I loved playing the "Mix these paints and see what colour we'll get, it'll be reyyyt!" game.

Now I am also no colour-palette-knowledgeable artist…

So on occasions, we ended up with some very questionable colours for certain rooms.

A glaringly bright 1980s custardy yellow adorned one hallway.

But it wasn't as bad as the hideous minty green toothpaste-y chaos that one bedroom ended up painted with!

Even I was glad when the tenant covered that up with a dinosaur mural!

Thankfully, those dodgy paints ran out, and since then, I now simply whiteout all the rooms, perhaps with one coloured feature wall on a chimney breast if we feel brave.

White walls and ceilings are fresh, bright and airy, and are literally a blank canvas.

Dodgy decor is soooo last season - so choose your colours wisely!

I've admitted before: I'm not very good at visualising things that aren't there.

So when it comes to planning out where electrical sockets and switches should go, in terms of planning out where the future imaginary furniture would be in a house: mistakes, I've made a few!

Yes, I've had light switches put on the wrong side of the door, so it opens onto the switch instead of next to it.

Yes, I've not added enough plug sockets to rooms and had to have more retrofitted afterwards.

The worst mistake I made was putting a switch for a hallway inside a HMO room, with the intention of converting that bit of hallway into a self-contained unit kitchen bit… until I realised that I would then be billed for two sets of council tax, so I scrapped that plan.

But it was too late! The electrician had followed my orders, and now that hallway -missing-switch-cos-it's-in-that-room bit annoys me every time I see it!

If you're not earning, you're learning, right?!

Here’s the final property mistake I won’t be repeating, one I definitely learnt my lesson from… the first and only time I did it!

In a house of multiple occupancy, we were bringing a new room into use.

My beloved Mummio was helping, in the days before we started employing professional fitters - she’s a dab hand at laying the odd carpet in the odd (easily square!) room.

I was sent out to get a carpet for said large room.

Did I go for a high-quality, hard-wearing, decently thick and lovely textured carpet?

No: I went purely on price and got a cheap, thin, corduroy-type carpet, at a bargain price of just £39.

And when she saw the utter cheap tat I had bought and brought back, she went absolutely nuts.

“Look how thin this crap is, it’s like bleeding paper, I can cut it with scissors it’s that thin. Don’t buy this sh!t again, we’re not having it.”

And that was me duly told.

But of course, she was right, because not only was it thin and poor quality, it wrinkled and ruffled up once on the floor.

So I never bought cheap crap carpets again!

That’s why we don’t buy cheap rubbish, ladies and gentlemen, it’s false economy - you get what you pay for!

If nowt else, get better quality stuff just to save the earache and stop your mum whining!

Remember… nobody gets everything right first time every time.

Mistakes are all part of learning, so embrace them – and learn what those mistakes teach you!

The Benefits of Renting to Tenants on Benefits!

You might know that I have a property rental portfolio here in Leeds.

What you might not know is that half of my single let rentals are occupied by tenants on benefits.

Now whilst benefits tenants often get a bad reputation, many low-income families are just like you and me: decent, pleasant people, that have found themselves in a certain situation.

Being on benefits does not mean that you are a write-off, or a bad person. It does not mean you are scum, a degenerate, a waster, or any of the other negative connotations the media try to impose on us.

Of course, there are some people who aren't as savoury as we would hope, throughout all areas of life - but we cannot tar everyone with the same brush.

Not all benefits tenants are bad ones, in the same surprising way that not all high paid 'professional tenants' look after the property and pay their rent - as some of my other landlord friends will vouch for!

As with anybody, carefully check out your prospective tenants, and be convinced that they are a good choice.

Here's my reasons for the benefits of renting to tenants on benefits:

- ✳ They are usually families, looking for a long-term home, which means they stay longer.
- ✳ There are lots of them looking for housing, as the council has a severe shortage of available local housing authority accommodation.
- ✳ Often the council will provide a deposit for them or a scheme whereby they will fix damaged items
- ✳ You can request for the rent to be paid directly to yourself as landlord. This massively reduces the risk of rent not getting paid.
- ✳ You are helping vulnerable families by giving them a chance to build themselves a secure lifestyle, and a steady foundation for their children to progress in the future…

… because that's exactly what happened to me.

I'm the product of a single parent on benefits. And although we were poor, our council house was immaculate, and we tried hard to improve our situation.

I'm not scum, a reprobate, a degenerate, a lowlife, or any of those things.

I'm a good person, just like my tenants are.

I was a kid who had a good grounding to want to do better than the situation I found myself in.

I appreciate everything, because I still remember what it means to have nothing.

And that's exactly why I choose to rent to low-income families - because I've been there, and know how important is it for someone to just give you a chance and believe in you.

So as there's over 3 million people claiming housing benefit in Britain… why not consider renting to them?!?

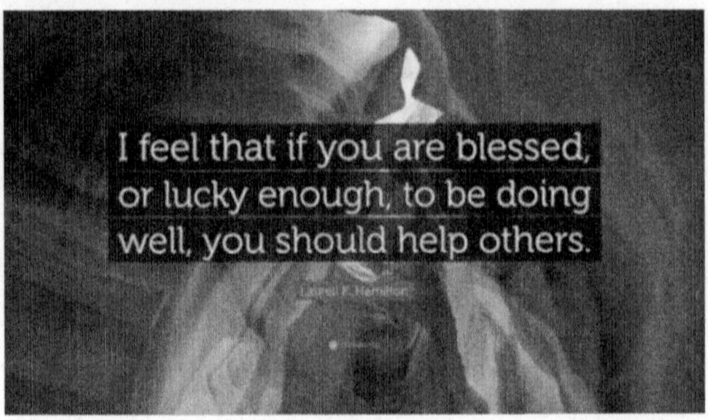

10 YEARS OF LANDLORDING - ...and Ten Things I've learned about being a Landlord in the that time!

Somehow, somewhere, over a full decade has passed since I first rented out a property!

In late 2008, I moved into a house, and kept my little cheap cheerful flat I'd lived in since 2001.

I rented it out to a nice single older chappy who kept it superbly tidy - and realised pretty quickly: “This is great! The mortgage is getting paid and I’m making some money on top of that as well!

It would be a few more years though until I started building my portfolio properly - shame it wasn’t ten years earlier!

Nevertheless, when I hit a decade of being a landlord, I reflected on the things I’d learned about ‘landlording’ over the previous ten years, and thought I would share my thoughts so they help other new landlords.

Obviously now I’ve got a few extra years added to my belt, but the lessons still remain the same…

So here goes!

1. TENANTS ON BENEFITS AND YOUR GUT INSTINCT

Just because a tenant is on benefits it doesn't make them a bad choice. If someone is a wretch, it is because they are a wretch, not because they are on benefits. I have a couple of benefits families and they are great, and I'm glad I didn't rule them out.

However, if your gut instinct tells you a potential tenant is a wretch, your gut instinct is right.

In ten years, I have only rented to two different people that turned out badly – and I had a bad feeling about both them as soon as I met them.

Still, I didn't listen to my gut, decided to give them a chance in my multi-let property – and both times, they caused me problems, chaos and lost rent. But luckily, they were short-lived and ejected reasonably swiftly after a bit of fuss.

And my gut instinct said afterwards; "Ha! I told you so! Should've listened!"

2. NOBODY CARES ABOUT YOUR PROPERTY AS MUCH AS YOU

Not even letting agents – they're not worried if you're losing money because it's not their house and it's not their money!

Items that have previously annoyed me about letting agents include:

Ripping me off for organising basic repairs. £100 for a gas safety certificate? Ahahahahahahah!!! Nah, you're alright love, I'll book a guy mysen!

Charging me hundreds of pounds for what is effectively a ten-minute job reprinting paperwork

Not informing me about issues with the property (more details later…)

Sourcing for me what turned out to be an unsuitable tenant who obviously had debt problems – why didn't they pick that up? It's not like I didn't pay them an…

EXTORTIONATE amount for their referencing!

Not managing to find me a suitable tenant for a rental, leaving me with a void of four months – FOUR MONTHS! And these are supposed to be the professionals! (Incidentally, when they left, I found a new tenant myself, who moved in within 13 DAYS!)

Trapping you in a contract forevermore, so that even if they're rubbish, it'll still cost you a month's rent to leave them.

My final peeve is their extortionate fees for very little work. At the time of writing, I only had one property left contracted / trapped with an agent – my little flat – and every month the letting agent collected the rent into their bank account and simply transferred it to my bank account – and charged me £42.72 every month for the privilege.

Thanks for that, really great value!

Now listen, I'm not saying all letting agents are terrible, lazy, a waste of money etc etc.

They are definitely useful if you live miles away from the property, or don't want to deal with any of the rental hassles that occur.

I am open to working with awesome letting agents in the future, if such a thing exists, whereby they are fair, proactive, reasonably priced and can do the job better than me.

Do let me know if you find said unicorn!

3. MAINTENANCE ISSUES NEVER ARISE ON THEIR OWN!

There is some magic law of Landlord Land, that across the portfolio, things never go wrong in isolation.

Maintenance issues never arise on their own, one thing at a time - they get shy about making themselves known, and talk to their naughty issue mates, so that magically there's always a couple of things that happen together.

Nowt happens for ages, and then suddenly a boiler will break, some wretch will fire an air rifle pellet at a window and then a ceiling will cave in from a floor leak upstairs. All at once.

This is some sort of evil maintenance Sod's law!

So prepare for this multi-chaos, it's very stressful, and painful to the wallet.

4. TENANTS ARE YOUR CUSTOMERS

Without tenants, you have no customers and so they should be treated politely and fairly, if you expect the same treatment in return.

Why wouldn't you look after them if you want them to remain in your house, looking after it, and paying rent?!
It boils my blood to hear about wretch landlords who don't look after their tenants.

I've taken a family on whose previous residence was black with mould: the landlord did nothing and the kiddy has asthma.

Not fair, not acceptable, and whilst I admit I'm far from perfect, at least I'm trying to do a good job. These landlord wretches are making us good landlords look bad!

5. YOU SHOULD BE HAPPY TO LIVE IN YOUR OWN HOUSES

If I wouldn't live in certain conditions, I don't expect my tenants to. This applies to safety features, decor, everything.

Several times after a refurbishment I've said: this is better than my own house! (And usually much bigger!)
Be thinking: is this acceptable? How can I make it better?
Be responsible and ethical.

Accidents don't just happen, they are caused - by negligence. Minimise risk for the tenants. Ask yourself what's the worst thing that could happen if I don't resolve this issue?
And my big conscience pricking thought is always "Ooooh, what if this happens and it hurts the kiddy?!"

I wouldn't be able to live with myself, and I like to sleep at night: so make sure you do the right thing.

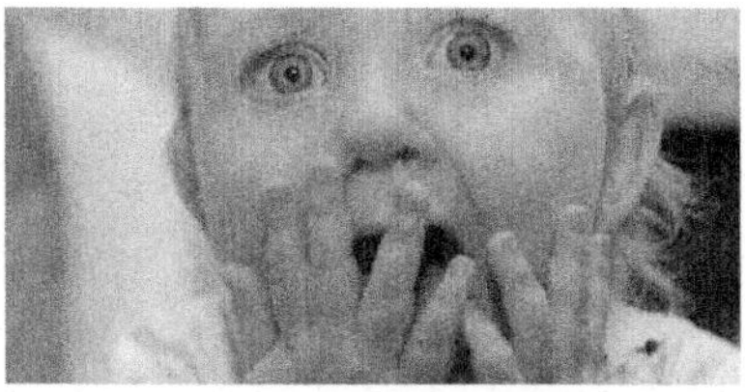

6. FIX MAINTENANCE ISSUES QUICKLY

If an issue arises, it doesn't go away!

In a lot of cases, they get worse if you don't deal with them, so fix issues quickly. Once a tenant started getting damp in flat from a leak on the balcony, and reported it to the letting agent – who did nothing, least of all inform me.

By the time the tenant got fed up and decided to complain to me directly, after about 8 months, the issue had gotten much worse. A great deal of damp mould had developed over that time, and it cost me much more to put it right than it would have done if the agents had told me when they should have done. Ballbags.

Lessons to be learned from this: encourage tenants to highlight issues early. Some don't, bafflingly, for fear you'll get annoyed with them (!!)

One crazy example that still bewilders me is this: On an inspection, the tenant let me in the side door telling me it was because the front door had stopped opening a couple of months earlier. Hence my horror: "Why didn't you tell me? How will you get out if there's a fire? You're eight months' pregnant!!"

I have a conscience, but through no fault of my own, if all had gone horrendously wrong, I could have ended up in jail…

Another lesson – inspect the property yourself frequently to check all is well.

7. GET THE PAPERWORK RIGHT

Do the paperwork documents properly and professionally. They protect you if anything goes wrong. And if you don't know what to do, learn!

Things to consider:

Assured Shorthold Tenancy Agreement
Right to Rent Checks
Credit Checks and Referencing
Inventory of the property
Copy of the Government's 'How to Rent' Guide
Gas Safety Certificate
The electricity and gas meter readings
Information about Government-approved Tenancy Deposit Scheme.
Tenancy Deposit Registration
Energy Performance Certificate
Electrical Inspection Record and Electrical Safety Certificates
Contact details for the Landlord
Smoke alarms, heat detectors and carbon monoxide alarms
Rent collection details
Deed of Surrender at the end of a tenancy

8. REMEMBER THAT BOTH TENANTS AND LANDLORDS ARE HUMANS

Because we are people, things sometimes happen in our lives that are not great.

Be understanding - but not a mug.

Learn the difference between someone who is having genuine hardship issues and work with them to come up with a solution.

If you encourage them to always be honest with you when an issue arises, you can work through it together.

An example of this might be: “My boss has had a payroll problem and my wage hasn’t gone in yet, sorry, my rent will be a few days late.”

I am fine when people are honest with me and tell me that they are working their way to a solution. As long as it doesn't happen too often!

However, on the other hand, some people are just full of bullshit.

Some tenants tell you outright lies that would make Pinocchio blush.

Work out when someone is just trying to take the piss out of you.

Then deal with them appropriately!

And remember: people treat you exactly how you allow them to.

I remember one time, the aforementioned debt tenants (sourced by those pesky letting agents!) - both working, and both on a couple of packs of expensive cigarettes a day - said me that they were struggling to afford the rent - so would I reduce the rent by £100 a month?!

What?!
Are you joking?!!

Would my own mortgage company accept that cheeky proposal?

Like a broken bit of rope: I'm a frayed knot.

I'm not a charity, and I have my own bills to pay.

So although they were nice people, they had to move somewhere more affordable.

And their many debt-chasing letters still go to the house now, several years later.

Sad, but you're not responsible for the way other people conduct their affairs. So don't be a mug about it!

9. BE CLEAR TO TENANTS ON EXPECTATIONS

Tenants have a wide, varying spectrum of opinions on what is 'acceptable' - in terms of cleanliness, behaviour, and especially at the end of a tenancy "returning the property back in a lettable state".

Give them clear guidelines of what is expected and what is not tolerated.

My most recent example is on a tenant changeover. I did indeed give them a list of what was required, including a requirement to have it professionally cleaned. (Which they ignored!)

They had cleared the house, but not cleaned it; it was filthy, but worse of all stank throughout. I had to say to her: "I can't rent it out again like that, the whole house stinks of dog piss!".

And she replied "Ohhh, I thought you'd say that…" REALLY?!?!!

A neighbour informed us why, after they left: apparently, they had had several dogs instead of the one they were allowed. Thus, every floor covering, pristinely laid brand new at the beginning of the tenancy 3.5 years earlier, had to be ripped up and replaced. All the house had to be scrubbed and repainted.

Tenant deposit, which they most definitely did not get back: £650.
Total cost to myself to put house back to a lettable state: £1069.01.

Lessons learned, which I have since implemented:

Don't leave a landlord inspection more than a year!

Give standards sheet at beginning of tenancy and when they give their notice. Remind them it needs to be exactly how it was when they moved in.

Note on inventory smell of rooms, plus condition of items, i.e., brand new/ installed May of year 2022 etc.

Do a video tour inventory as well – difficult to dispute something they see on screen. Send them this when they hand in their notice.

Give them a Pet Policy with clear guidelines.

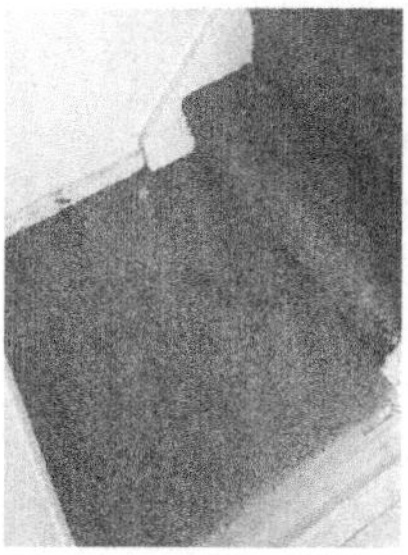

10. THE BEST THING ABOUT BEING A LANDLORD?

You genuinely have the power to improve someone else's life by providing them with a home.
There's no better feeling for me than handing someone keys to their new home when they previously had nowhere.

You are enabling them to have a stabilising factor in making their life better.

So despite all the chaos, paperwork, stress, maintenance, costs, and occasional tenant issues, there's a very good reason that I, and many other landlords do this line of work.

We're helping people!

YOUR NEXT STEPS...

Well, what now?

You've read my entire book, so if you've not been put off by property, how do you go about starting your own property career?

Here's the guidance, in a very particular order:

Work out why you want to do property, even after knowing why, it is hard. Be honest with yourself – because not many people do it for the pure love of bricks and mortar.

Is it because you want a change, or more time, freedom, money, to create a legacy, or something else?

The more honest and specific the reason, the better likelihood you'll have of achieving it.

Decide how dedicated you are to achieving it.

It's not an easy, get-rich quick scheme. You won't be a millionaire in five seconds with no work.
Nobody is, it's futile wishful thinking.

You will have to put in some hard graft to begin with.

Do the work, Kiss a lot of frogs. Fail. Make mistakes. Fail again. You'll have sleepless nights, worries, anxiety, panic, and a constant fear you're a fraud, you'll go broke, you're a failure, it'll all go wrong, you're not good enough, etc etc etc.

If you're of a nervous disposition, or to be brutal, you know you're quite lazy… quite frankly, you'd be better off sticking to a normal job providing security exchanging your time for money under somebody else's management.

Brutally harsh?
Yep.
Realistic and honest?
Also yep.

"But I've got funds", I hear you say…

Have you realised that you've got the money for property, but not the time, knowledge or inclination to deal with property yourself?

It's ok, I get it!

That's exactly why armchair angel investors exist, and if you'd like to be one of my angel investors on my property projects, visit my website to find out more:
www.kellyannmartin.co.uk

Still here?
Ok, we press on!

Research research research property before you part with any money. Learn the market, the tactics, the property strategies, the area you want to operate in, and your own personal comfort level and risk profile.

I am happy to send you on a free property beginner's course to give you some guidance, with the very same people I learned my craft from - just email me on hello@kellyannmartin.co.uk and ask me to book you a free place.

Make a plan, and write it down - because without writing it down in words, it's just some faraway wish in your head.

A goal without a plan is just a dream.

So this plan – which you must write down! - should consist of your vision, your objectives, your mission of what you are trying to achieve, and your action plan – where, when and how you are going to achieve it. Now here's the hard bit which requires stamina, dedication, guts, and getting uncomfortable – do what you are telling yourself to do in the plan…

Take some action, and be consistent with it.
Do what you know you should do, the things you've been taught to do in the process.

Do it over and over again, even when the going gets tough, and it feels like there's nothing happening.

Do the work, don't be lazy, and keep believing that it will happen.

I find that the harder I work, the luckier I get. Whereas when I do nothing, nothing happens.

KEEP GOING UNTIL YOU GET WHERE YOU WANT TO BE.

That literally is it. Sounds easy, sounds simple... but if it was as easy as that, everybody would do it... wouldn't they?!?

I wish you lots of luck as you embark on your property journey.

Embark is a good word to use, because like embarking on an epic sea voyage, it will be a rough and bumpy ride – and will definitely make you feel sick at times!

I've never once said it will be easy. But, as whenever you overcome anything difficult, it will always be worth it…

I would love to know how you get on, and my very best wishes for your future.

Kellyann Martin **x x x**

… just a very ordinary, normal girl from Leeds trying to make an honest living!

ACKNOWLEDGEMENTS

Thanks for reading – I hope it helps you plan out your future!

If you've found this book beneficial, do please leave a review and recommend it to others.

Meanwhile, some acknowledgements of my gratitude…

I'd like to say a massive thank you to everyone that has helped along the way in my property investment journey.

They say no man (woman?!) is an island, and it really has been made much easier by having other people involved in making things happen.

To all my lovely angel investors, hardworking and professional contractors – thank you making my property visions reality.

To my friends, family, colleagues, mentors and followers of my work – thank you for providing positive encouragement, support and guidance. I am so grateful for your support.

Finally, a very special mention to my Mummio, my Doggio, and my Favourite Personio – thank you for everything you do, and for always putting up with my nonsense and shenanigans - it is you who reminds me why I'm doing this! ♥♥♥

I can help you grow your wealth.
Our property investments are secure and low-risk.
Investment short-term, with an excellent fixed rate return.
We put in knowledge, skills, education, effort, network, time, and project management.
This means your investment is totally hands-free!
- Kellyann Martin
#mybeautifulLeeds

Printed in Great Britain
by Amazon

81483927R00129